RETHINKING RACISM

RETHINKING RACISM

EMOTION, PERSUASION, AND LITERACY
EDUCATION IN AN ALL-WHITE HIGH SCHOOL

Jennifer Seibel Trainor

Southern Illinois University Press / Carbondale

11 10 09 08   4 3 2 1

Library of Congress Cataloging-in-Publication Data
Trainor, Jennifer S., 1968–
Rethinking racism : emotion, persuasion, and literacy edu-
cation in an all-white high school / Jennifer Seibel Trainor.
        p. cm.
Includes bibliographical references and index.
ISBN-13: 978-0-8093-2873-4 (pbk. : alk. paper)
ISBN-10: 0-8093-2873-9 (pbk. : alk. paper)
1. Racism in education—United States—Case studies.
2. Multicultural education—United States—Case studies.
3. Anti-racism—Study and teaching (Secondary)—United
States—Case studies. I. Title.
LC212.T73 2008
371.82900973—dc22   2008010204

Printed on recycled paper. ♻
The paper used in this publication meets the minimum
requirements of American National Standard for Informa-
tion Sciences—Permanence of Paper for Printed Library
Materials, ANSI Z39.48-1992. ∞

CONTENTS

ACKNOWLEDGMENTS

I am grateful to many colleagues and friends who aided me as I wrote this book. Among them are the following colleagues at the University of Pittsburgh who enlivened me with conversation and friendship, and whose confidence in me helped more than they know: Kathryn Flannery, Marah Gubar, Paul Kameen, Kellie Robertson, and Jim Seitz. I thank especially Dave Bartholomae for his mentorship and his belief in me and this project. I don't think I could have done it without his encouragement; I have benefited from ongoing conversations, collaborations, and friendship with Amanda Godley, whose writing and social justice convictions have always been a model for me. I am grateful to Cathy Prendergast for her feedback and help with this project, and to Julie Lindquist, whose work gave me new ways to think about persuasion and belief. Thanks also to Jabari Mahiri and to Glynda Hull, who helped me formulate my ideas for this project and who always pointed me in the right direction. Michelle Burnham, Eileen Elrod, and Jo Keroes generously read portions of the book and provided much-needed feedback and editing. I thank Vicki Botnick for her many years of friendship and support, and especially Kathy Newman, who tirelessly read drafts and talked me through the hard work of writing.

I thank Anne DiPardo, the editor at *Research in the Teaching of English*, whose incisive and patient feedback on an essay I published there helped me clarify my ideas. I am grateful to reviewers at Southern Illinois University Press and at *College Composition and Communication* for their insightful reading of the manuscript. Thanks to NCTE for permission to reprint my article "The Emotioned Power of Racism: An Ethnographic Portrait of an All-White High School" (*CCC*; copyright 2008 by the National Council of Teachers of English; used with permission), which appears in revised form as chapter 3. Many thanks also to Stuart Greene and Dawn Perkins, and to Peter Lang Publishers, for permission to reprint portions of chapter 5, which appeared in *Literacy as a Civil Right* (2008).

My deepest thanks to "Elizabeth Reed," whose real name cannot be revealed here for reasons of confidentiality, for generously allowing me into her classroom. Her insights and instincts as a teacher inform every page. Finally, I thank my family, especially my husband, Scott Trainor, on whose strength I have leaned for so long. This book is dedicated to him and to our son, Charlie.

Introduction
RACISM IN REAL TIME

It is raining, and class hasn't started. Students are chattering and laughing as they weave in between the hastily arranged clusters of desks. They seem more animated than usual, as if in protest against the muffling dampness outside. Chris slides into his desk and dumps his notebook down, a *Sports Illustrated* magazine on top. It's the one with Charles Barkley on the cover; Barkley is shackled in chains meant to evoke slavery, and the feature article is about racism in contemporary sports. "What a load of crap," Josh mutters as he walks by, glancing at the cover. He is soft-spoken and rarely talks in class. Like about a fourth of his classmates, he has been diagnosed with a mild learning disability, evidenced only by his thick, heavy glasses. Today he wears his usual uniform: western style long-sleeve buttoned-down shirt, jeans, a prominent belt buckle, and boots.

Tom concurs with Josh about the *Sports Illustrated* cover. He turns to me—I am a frequent confidant—and says softly, "What people don't understand, is that like you can't just reward people, who are lazy, you know? That's like what all of this does, affirmative action and welfare. It takes money and stuff from people who work hard and then like you give it to people who don't and then there's no incentive." A few other students are listening. Tom continues: "I'm not racist or anything, but did you know, like statistically, there are statistics that show, Black people are the laziest group?"

Tom attends Laurel Canyons High School, a public school about twenty miles from a midsized, mid-Eastern city. Laurel Canyons has a student population that is 97% white. Although classified as suburban, the school also serves a small rural population—including students like Josh, whose families live in small towns and on farms scattered around the area. The school sits on a hill accessible by a winding two-lane road that borders a golf course. On the east side of the road, just before the red-brick cluster of Laurel Canyons' buildings appears, there are six or seven tiny clapboard houses perched at the bottom of a steep embankment and almost out of

1

sight, tattered lawn chairs and fishing gear tangled on sagging porches just a few feet from a narrow creek. Across from the school is a flat-roofed, gym-sized structure that houses the First Word Baptist Church. A battered marquee announces youth group activities and Bible school classes.

Tom is fair-haired, tall, and angular. The identity poster he created during the first nine weeks of class is hanging on the far side of the room with those of his classmates. A large picture in the middle of it shows Tom in a hunting vest, rifle on one side, slain deer lying at his feet. "I will always work hard for my family," he wrote in the text portion of the poster. "I plan to go to college and learn to be a commercial airline pilot. I enjoy hunting, fishing, and messing around on the computer. My friends and family are the most important thing in my life." Tom lives with his parents—who, he tells me, worry that his politics are "too harsh"—in one of the new suburban communities that have sprung up in the district in the past several years. He's not rich, he says, like some of his classmates, who drive BMWs and live in gated housing developments. But he's not a "hick" either. In his opinion, the school has too many of those already.

Students continue to wander in. Some glance at the *Sports Illustrated* as they thread through the room, backpacks sliding off, bodies squeezing into blue plastic desks. I watch Michelle and Lisa, best friends since second grade, pull out their school-issued copies of Alice Walker's *The Color Purple*—its paperback cover shellacked into a hard surface for school and library use. They slap the books down on their desks in a practiced gesture of boredom and begin whispering. Warren is annoying everyone, weaving among the desks, commenting on his classmates' clothes, the weather, the game last week, his voice a hyperactive protest against the silence of the wet morning. He calls out a cheerful greeting to Julie, the inclusion teacher (there to provide instructional support for students, such as Warren and Josh, with learning disabilities). Elizabeth Reed, the official instructor for the class, has been teaching for seven years, all of them at Laurel Canyons. With her long hair, casual attire, and artistic sensibilities (she has decorated her classroom with reproductions of modern art, lists of favorite books and films, and flyers announcing local poetry readings and art exhibits), she is a magnet for sensitive, intellectual students. But this class is a general requirement, and though the students appreciate her liberal approach, many of them are neither motivated by the questions that animate her teaching nor inspired by the philosophy—of student empowerment, intellectual engagement, and social critique—that undergirds it. Warren is a case in point. When he notices the video equipment that has been wheeled in from technology services and is sitting on a cart behind the door, he points: "Hey everybody! TV! Mrs. Reed, do we get to watch the book on TV? Please say yes, say yes, say yes!"

None of the students whose desks are gathered near Tom's offers an objection to his opinion about the *Sports Illustrated* cover. But Chris, a good-natured student athlete with steady, intelligent blue eyes, shifts uncomfortably and begins to slide the magazine back into his backpack. Mike gives me an ironic grin as the magazine disappears. He turns to Tom but keeps one eye on me: "Dude, the Black people in this district are some of the wealthiest people there are. True, there are a lot who are lazy, but now they've learned to work it just like everybody else, and I guarantee you their house is bigger than yours."

I aim in this book to change the way we think about the causes and origins of white student racism. As the following pages document, such racism remains an urgent pedagogical problem, one that we have yet to fully understand. Indeed, such racism, I argue in this book, does not necessarily arise from a need or desire to protect white privilege, from ignorance of oppression, or from lack of exposure to difference. As long as the origins of racism are seen in these terms, curricular and pedagogical responses aimed at ameliorating racism—everything from multicultural exposure to difference to critical interrogations of whiteness and privilege—will be ineffective. Rather, I suggest instead that we understand racist discourses as a series of "emotioned" beliefs that are not necessarily about race per se. Students become convinced of such beliefs in part through the routines and culture of schooling, and they draw from them when confronted with matters of race, often with deleterious—that is to say, racist—effect. I use the term "emotioned" to suggest that such beliefs become persuasive through mediating and mediated processes of emotional regulation, individually experienced feelings, and dynamics of persuasion and rhetoric. While "emotional" suggests that such discourses relate causally to individual feelings—anger, hostility, fear—"emotioned" instead draws our attention to interconnected but nonlinear dynamics of lived affective experiences, emotional regulation taking place through institutional and cultural practices, and language. In this story of a year spent with the students at Laurel Canyons High School, I thus ask you to consider racism differently, to witness the ways in which Laurel Canyons students' racist assertions did not always or even often originate in racist attitudes or belief, and to see beyond the assumption that a racist assertion constitutes evidence of a student's racial ideology or political orientation. Instead, I invite you to consider that the persuasive appeal of racist discourses is affective and emotioned, rather than logical or rational, and that it is rooted not in abstract political or identity-based calculations but in local experiences and feelings that are given force in school.

In making this argument, I focus on the metaphoric functions of racist language, the ways it connects common racist ideas to nonracist feelings, values, beliefs, and associations that are often actually taught in school. Racist discourses, like Tom's above, are best understood as psychosocial rhetorical phenomena—forms of persuasion that need to be understood not only for their political meanings and implications but also for their persuasive subjective and affective coherence. Racist discourses structure feelings sometimes linked to, *but surprisingly rarely reducible to*, the racial politics such discourses forward. Seen through this lens, Tom is not protecting his white privilege or showing his ignorance of the struggles of African Americans in the United States, or even suffering from a lack of exposure to people of other races. Instead, we need to consider racist discourses like Tom's in light of what educational theorists have called the "hidden curriculum" of schooling—those tacit, taken-for-granted practices and rituals that scholars have linked to the teaching of social class identities—to see how school scaffolds emotioned frameworks within which racist discourses, such as Tom's, become persuasive. Thus I argue that part of what makes racist discourses persuasive is school itself—its many tacit, unexamined lessons, rituals, and practices that exert a powerful but largely unacknowledged pedagogical and persuasive force. In making this argument, I draw on recent scholarship on what Michalinos Zembylas (2005) calls emotional regimes: "aspects of school culture consisting of systems of emotional rules that [are] normatively imposed on members of the school" (474). If, as William Reddy (2001) writes, politics is about emotional control, "a process of determining who must repress as illegitimate, who must foreground as valuable, the feelings and desires that come up for them in given contexts and relationships" (1997, p. 335), then schools constitute an important arena for this process and must be investigated as such. In light of this and other recent research on emotion, I suggest both a new diagnosis of the causes of racism and a different approach to it: students' racism doesn't reduce to racism, a paradox I unpack throughout the book, and remedying it requires attention to the private, idiosyncratic, associative meanings of race for students, to the institutional contexts of schooling that inadvertently provide emotional scaffolding for racist discourses, and to the relationship between these two as they come together in the classroom.

I am not alone in calling for attention to emotion in our efforts to understand the workings of ideology. In *The Cultural Politics of Emotion* (2004), Sarah Ahmed bases her account of "how we become invested in social norms" (12) on the relationship between emotion and language, or what she calls "texts." Focusing in particular on metonymy and metaphor, she explores how language "gets stuck together" and "how sticking is dependent on past histories of association. . . . The emotionality of texts is one way of describing how texts are 'moving,' or how they generate effects." Indeed, she writes, the work of emotion involves the "sticking" of signs to bodies

(13). Beliefs, seen in this light, are "constituted through circulating signs and discourses that have been stuck together in a metonymic slide" (Rice 201–2). In composition, Gwen Gorzelky (2005) has also taken up questions of language, emotion, and social belief. She argues that changing ideologies is not a problem of demystification, critical consciousness, or indeed, philosophical work. Demystification functions only as an abstraction, and thus, Gorzelsky writes, it cannot access perception, which is structured by sensory and emotional processes. Blocked perception, she writes, cannot be freed through rational argument (29). Sharon Crowley (2006) similarly suggests, in her analysis of fundamentalist religious belief, that "emotions affect belief, and beliefs arouse emotion. Belief is stimulated, supported, or changed by emotional responses to an environment" (87). Crowley's argument suggests that antiracist educators have misplaced their energy on a "bloodless and cerebral" approach to argument, when they should be focused instead on the centrality of desires and values to the maintenance of beliefs (4), on the "moral and passionate commitment(s)" that constitute individuals' primary motivations and that govern how individuals respond to persuasive encounters within particular institutions and environments.

Rethinking Racism provides an analysis of those passionate commitments—like Tom's to the idea of a work ethic, as well as his negative emotioned response to "laziness"—and the institutional context that has given those commitments their force for Tom. For those of us who aim toward antiracism and social justice in our teaching, the resonant part of Tom's comment is its racism—the stereotyping of African Americans, the echoes of the nasty racism of the recent and distant American past. For Tom, the resonant portion of his comment is "laziness." This difference in perception helps explain the failure of our efforts to persuade Tom differently. Thus, at the heart of my analysis is a central insight into the nature of racism like Tom's: it originates in passions that are not about race per se (which, in Tom's case, are about determination and motivation versus laziness) but that are "elaborated"—to use Crowley's term. That is, they are made resonant for Tom and given force by pedagogical and institutional practices of schooling, which, at Laurel Canyons, are often centered on the importance of hard work to school success. These practices are called forth and misapplied, as it were, to what is for Tom the confusing and emotionally fraught topic of race.

In the pages that follow, I chronicle my observations of two English classes at Laurel Canyons over the course of a year: Advanced Writing, which served college-bound seniors, and Introduction to Humanities, a general graduation requirement that focused on introducing students to the humanities and providing support for them as they completed their senior projects. Both classes were taught by Elizabeth Reed, whom I chose to work with because of her commitment to critical pedagogy and her engagement with the challenges of antiracism with white students. You will hear, in the coming pages, many voices: those of teachers, administrators, and students, some hailing from affluent gated communities like the one where Mike lives, others who lived in suburban developments growing to the north of the school, and still others from dwindling rural and lower-middle-class townships on the edges of the district. Throughout the book, I describe student encounters with and responses to texts about race that range from contemptuous and confused to curious and compassionate. I chronicle lively class debates about stories such as *The Color Purple*. I attempt to capture students' informal talk about their schooling: their alienation, boredom, and cynicism, their curiosities and questions. I examine their writing and I analyze responses they gave during in-depth interviews, when I asked students to explain their ideas about texts that discussed race, to reflect on their learning about race, and to talk about their past experiences with multicultural literacy education.

The intertwined topics of race and literacy in public education have proven, in the past several years, to be difficult and contentious matters of public and academic debate. Arguments about what students should read and why they should read it recur frequently in the media, in local schools, and on college and university campuses. Within the academy, research has become increasingly focused on the social and political dimensions of reading and writing and on literacy as a social and cultural activity rather than a cognitive or individual one. In this view, literacy education teaches students not only value-neutral print encoding and decoding skills but also culturally endorsed values that range from socioeconomic class habits to gender identities and power relationships. The connections between literacy education and social, political, and economic forces have become, in this way, an integral part of pedagogical theory, classroom research, and to some extent, classroom practice. Literacy education is thus understood as a tool in the construction of consciousness—the shaping of particular kinds of identities in young people (Hunter 1988). It teaches students, as James Berlin writes, "how to interpret the world, how to experience it, what emotions to have, what values to adopt" (Berlin 1996, 178).

The view of literacy that Hunter, Berlin, and others articulate has made educators increasingly aware of the potential of curricular and pedagogical choices to shape students' values in progressive ways, with the resulting proliferation of critical, feminist, antiracist, multicultural, and liberatory pedagogies. But subsequent research on and much anecdotal lore among teachers about antiracist education, including multiculturalism and pedagogies that interrogate white privilege, suggest that such efforts have consistently fallen short with white students. Much of this research posits a characterization of white students as privileged—benefiting from an unjust racial hierarchy in the United States—and therefore as unwilling to engage with texts or ideas that critique privilege or suggest the need for social change. *Rethinking Racism* sets this notion on its head. It turns the focus away from structures of privilege and their effects on white students' beliefs and toward structures of emotion as they are taught via the institutional practices of literacy, including critical and multicultural literacy, toward an integrated theory of persuasion, emotions, and institutions as a way to understand white racism and ultimately to change it.

To understand how institutions work on emotions and how emotions in turn work on beliefs about race, I turned to one of the most carefully calibrated and overdetermined institutions in the United States, the high school. As David Larabee (1997) writes, high schools are among only a few institutions in the U.S. where the values of a society are explicitly taught, learned, and practiced. In addition, of course, high schools are part of composition's "extracurriculum"; they represent one of many important sites of literacy work outside the university, though obviously central to such work (Gere 1994). A span of only three months' time separates some of the students in this study from the freshmen that those of us in composition work with each fall. Much of the frustration that has characterized scholarship in composition around antiracist, critical teaching stems from our efforts to enact such pedagogies in freshmen classes. In my own teaching, I have often felt that I needed a deeper understanding of where my students come from—not in the narrow sense of understanding what has "been covered" in terms of curriculum or what students might be expected already to know but rather an understanding of the rhetorical communities and institutions and social networks they have grown up in and that, during the fall of their freshman year, they have not fully disentangled themselves from. The field of composition has given us ethnographies of the language and literacy practices of Alcoholics Anonymous (Daniell 2003) and of a working-class tavern in Chicago (Lindquist 2002), as well as analyses of college students' oral performances and out-of-school literacy practices (Fishman and Lunsford 2005), to name just a few of the studies that take us beyond the borders of the freshman classroom. A study of high school literacy practices, conducted with an eye toward understanding particular concerns that have animated composition, can illuminate our field and its questions in new and productive ways. There are, of course, many studies of high schools written by and for scholars in education and for practicing K–12 teachers. I drew heavily on this scholarship as I conducted my research at Laurel Canyons. But in my analysis, and as I wrote about my experiences, I kept the field of composition squarely in mind, with the aim of making this important, closely related site of literacy illuminate some of the questions we have asked in composition studies about racism and critical teaching.

Elizabeth caught my eye as Warren pleaded to "watch the book on TV." He got his wish. The day's agenda included viewing two scenes from Steven Spielberg's film based on Walker's novel. I gave Elizabeth a smile back, and she shrugged, her small face lifted in tolerant amusement: if you can't beat 'em, join 'em. She knows that most of the kids have not read past the first ten pages of the novel. It's boring, they tell her, and weird. But Elizabeth is one of those teachers who will do what it takes to engage her students. Film and popular culture are much more powerful in their lives than books are. On the bulletin board she has tacked up lists of her favorite movies: *Buffalo 66, Alice's Restaurant, Smoke Signals, Educating Rita*. If Spielberg could spark some discussion or maybe generate enough curiosity to get the kids to read a little further, well, that was the point, wasn't it? She relied on quizzes and other more coercive assignments like journal entries with page requirements only when the curriculum required her to. In general, she thought these approaches encouraged cheating and cultivated a cynical view, whereas she wanted to open her students up to the world of ideas.

"Yes Warren, we're going to watch TV. Ya happy now?" she joked, wheeling the cart to the front of the room, gesturing for students to move desks and backpacks so that all could see the screen. She was a serious teacher, but she enjoyed the kids too; she was interested in their gossip and moved by their struggles. Her planning periods were punctuated by frequent visits from students wanting to tell their tales to a sympathetic ear. Yesterday it was Brian who lumbered into her room as she and I sat reading through students' journals and talking about possible writing assignments. Brian was over six feet tall, stoop-shouldered, round-faced, with a crop of brown curls and long-fingered gentle hands that belied his size. He was also gay, one of the few students in the school who was "out," and he had a crush on a boy who wasn't. Elizabeth was his confidant. "She's a wonderful teacher," he said, when Elizabeth introduced me. "She's been so important to me, when I'm like the only gay person in this totally homophobic school."

As Elizabeth prepared the VCR, the room began to hum with talk. "Why doesn't she just give us a test on this?" Mike complained to the students sitting near him. "I can b.s. my way through a test. But an essay, writing, you have to go on and on."

Nate snorted and began to imitate a teacher: "Don't you want to express your thoughts about the book?" There was laughter. Nate rivaled Warren for the official title of class clown.

"Why should I!" Mike said. "It's not going to help me. I'll never need to know about it on the job. I just need it to get an A so I can get this over with. Reading this book will take me a week. Watching the movie will take two hours. Why would I want to read about some lesbian living in the 1600s? Do you know how much money I could earn if I spent that time at my job?"

Chris pretended to calculate: "Let's see, you earn, what, a big three dollars an hour at Abercrombie, and you work maybe ten hours at that crappy drive-through on the weekends, so I'd say, maybe nothing?"

Two student coordinators for one of the extracurricular clubs came in. They conferred in whispers with Elizabeth, who said to the class, "Hey guys, we have some people here who want to talk to you about volunteering."

The two girls stood at the front of the class. "Hi. We're from S.A.D.D. [Students Against Destructive Decisions], and our group does a lot of presentations in the grade schools about student choice and making good choices," the first girl said. Every fourth or fifth word rose to a question pitch. "And we raise money for drug education. You can make a team with other students, or maybe your church youth group, and compete to raise money for this charity. You get color-coded T-shirts for your team." They passed around a sign-up sheet. As it went around the room, Nate, Chris, and Mike continued to talk about grades.

"I cannot fail English," Nate said. "How many points do you guys have?

"I've got 158."

"What's your grade in here now?"

"I think 158 is a B"

"I've got 77."

"That's not failing. You'll get 40 points just for the journals when she hands them back."

Elizabeth raised her teacher's voice above the din. "Thank you, Lisa and Amy," she said to the coordinators, who collected their sign-up sheet and headed for the door. "Let's talk a little bit about *The Color Purple* before we watch these two scenes. Get out your reading responses." There was a shuffle of papers and a slight lowering of voices, but the talking continued. "Anybody want to read from what they wrote?"

Warren, who starts almost every discussion, shot up his hand like an elementary school student and bounced a little bit in his seat to get Elizabeth's attention.

"Yes, Warren." Elizabeth said. The room got a little more quiet.

"I feel like the first page was very disturbing," Warren reported to the class. There was nodding. Some students began to flip through the first pages of their books.

"The first page is too open for me," Michelle said cryptically.

"She's writing to God and I couldn't understand what she's saying."

"They're like journal entries," Elizabeth attempted to clarify.

"The way she writes," Michelle persisted. "It's just gibberish. You can't understand a word she's saying. It's not English to me. The way they word stuff, the way she spells stuff. It's not proper English."

"Okay, good. That's a good observation, Michelle. Let's look at the time period. In the early 1900s. Were Black children educated then? Does anybody know?"

"How are we supposed to know she's Black?" someone asked from the back of the room.

Nate made a disgusted sound, hissing through his teach. "It's pretty obvious she's not rich and white."

"By page 20, she's fourteen and talking about getting married. Dude that's crazy!"

"The whole situation is disgusting to me," Michelle said. "A father and daughter. This book is pornographic!"

Tom agreed. "I think it's too graphic," he said softly. "It's vulgar." He shook his head. "I don't think we should be reading books like that."

Joel said, too softly for the whole class or Elizabeth to hear, "I felt like a fag carrying that book around. It's a chick's book, you know, the cover."

Mike sighed. "I hate reading about poor people."

Listening to Laurel Canyons students was often troubling for me and for Elizabeth. But at their most troubling—when Tom condemns *The Color Purple* as "too graphic," when Joel says the novel makes him feel "like a fag," when Michelle protests that the Black English in the novel is "not proper English"—they suggest much more than ignorance, prejudice, lack of exposure to difference, or an excess of white privilege. To capture these responses to matters of race, to situate them within institutional and emotioned contexts, and to come to see them, as I did, as arising from unintentionally racialized lessons learned in school, required the dimension of history afforded me by my year-long participation in the life of the school. To trace Michelle's hostility toward Black English to her own alienation from what she perceived to be the school's hyperfocus on correctness, to see how such attitudes, though racist when they are applied, for example, to Walker's novel, were actually learned in other, seemingly nonracialized places in the institutional and pedagogical world of Laurel Canyons, required time. I went to Elizabeth's classes every morning for one academic year and watched students' learning and thinking unfold across the arc of school-structured time: September, midyear grade reports, snow days, holidays, prom, senior projects, graduation. I try to capture this unfolding by telling a story that is anchored in a sense of chronology: I begin my story in its multiple beginnings—in my own history with questions about race and teaching, and in the fall of the school year I spent at Laurel Canyons—and I end in June, as graduation neared.

But this is a chronology figured in a number of unconventional ways: for example, my story is also about students' early memories of racial learning, what I call "beginning stories," told to me in interviews during which I asked how they first learned about the issues that came up in the multicultural texts they read. It is about students' first responses to texts about race and the new ideas about race these texts introduced. It is about Elizabeth's reflections on her experiences at Laurel Canyons, gleaned from interviews two years after she quit her position there. It is also about my own racial learning as a white antiracist educator and researcher, about my memories of race, and about what I have learned about it over the course of this research. Finally, in its blend of narrative with more traditional forms of ethnographic analysis, the book is about how constructions of racism originate—in literacy research and in our classrooms—and how those constructions themselves can limit the rhetorical positions students enact. Like Gorzelsky, I am interested in the narratives and allegories underlying our ethnographies. As she writes, "ethnography can't directly represent reality but [it] can—and should—evoke the possibility of a more equitable, just community" (6). And like Gorzelsky, I use explicitly rhetorical and literary strategies to make my text's form a part of its argument (6).

For example, each chapter is differently oriented around beginnings and endings, as I trace discourses about race to their origins in students' emotioned experiences in school, and each chapter is filtered through the experiences of four students: Mike, Michelle, Laura, and Ashley, who will be introduced more fully in the pages ahead. Chapter 1, "Racism, Persuasion, and Emotion: Reflections on Then and Now," describes key terms on which the arguments in subsequent chapters rest and provides a kind of intellectual history of the project—narrating how my views of the terms of this book have changed over time, through the course of this research. In this chapter, I create a framework for understanding racism as an emotioned response governed by the structure and practices of school.

Chapter 2, "Class Beginnings: September and October," describes the ethnographic context of this research and my research methodology. Here I introduce the focal students, using narratives drawn from the beginning of the school year that highlight the emotional tenor of many classroom discussions of race and that suggest the interplay between the everyday practices of school and racism. These narratives also complicate representations, in the scholarship on racism, of whiteness as privileged, dominant, or advantaged. They unravel the notion that racism is both a result and a cause of white privilege, and they layer abstractions about privilege and whiteness with contradictory and locally specific meanings.

Chapter 3, "Emotioned Rules Taught in School and the Persuasive Power of Racism: November and December," unpacks the "emotioned rules" (a term I borrow from Michalinos Zembylas's 2005 essay on poststructuralist views of emotion and identity) undergirding social and literate practices at Laurel Canyons. It examines how these rules supported the racist discourses students often relied on, and gave these discourses their persuasive power. Engaging recent theories of the social dimensions of emotion, this chapter illustrates how taken-for-granted school and literate practices, as well as the emotioned rules embedded within them, created a rhetorical framework in the classroom within which racism became persuasive. In this chapter I build on research on "the hidden curriculum" and social class identity formation in order to show how elements of the hidden curriculum at Laurel Canyons also taught emotions that inadvertently gave racist discourses their force.

While chapters 2 and 3 explore different kinds of beginnings, moving chronologically from the literal beginning of the school year through early spring and tracing the origins of racist discourses across time and contexts, chapters 4 and 5 are centered on different kinds of endings. In chapter 4, "When to Break the Rules: February, March, and April," I continue the kind of analysis I began in chapter 3, this time examining the emotioned rules embedded in the critical and multicultural pedagogies Elizabeth employed. If in the previous chapter we saw how students' racism was upheld, even promoted, by emotioned rules enforced in school, this chapter shows how teachers' efforts to disrupt racism are stymied by an incomplete engagement with and understanding of how emotions work in the context of antiracist persuasion. This chapter draws in part on an interview with Elizabeth conducted two years after my research ended. At that point, Elizabeth had left Laurel Canyons for another teaching job in a high school with a more rigorous intellectual climate and a more upper-middle-class student population. In that interview Elizabeth reflected on her struggles to teach at Laurel Canyons. She commented on individual students' emotional development, and she talked at length of her frustration with the constraints imposed by the culture of schooling—the need to keep parents happy, the imperatives of state curricular guidelines, the insistence of other teachers, students, and administrators that she adjust her goals to the routine practices of a suburban public high school. In that interview, I found the beginnings of my analysis of racism at Laurel Canyons.

Chapter 5 chronicles the last few months at Laurel Canyons, as students finished their senior projects (a high-stakes graduation requirement) and prepared for graduation. Titled "Beyond White Privilege: June at Laurel Canyons," this chapter draws from critical race theory's notion of whiteness as wage, investment, or property, a formulation given particular force by Catherine Prendergast's (2003) analysis of white investment in literacy. I offer reflections on the emotioned dimensions of white investments in literacy and conclude with a discussion of what attention to emotion can offer teachers and researchers as they develop persuasive antiracist rhetorics for the classroom. All chapters contain narrative descriptions of classroom interactions, rhetorical and ethnographic analysis of racist discourses, and essayist reflections on the literature about antiracism and critical teaching. These mixed genres form what Deborah Hicks (2002) calls a "hybrid language of inquiry" (136).

"She circled 'colored,'" Mike said, when he got his journal on *The Color Purple* back from Elizabeth. "I must have misspelled it." He handed me his notebook.

"No," I said. "That's how you spell it. But that's not really the right term." I faltered for a moment, trying to think about how to explain.

"I should say 'African American,'" Mike offered, filling in the silence.

"You could put 'Black,'" Chris suggested.

"But that's politically incorrect," Tom said, as if political incorrectness would earn the same deduction in points as misspellings or grammar mistakes.

Mike turned to me. "I don't really get this whole African American thing. Because they're not African Americans. They're Americans. Like I'm German American, but I don't go around saying I'm German American. I'm just American. Because if they want to live back in Africa, why don't they just go? Or they should go with the American part and just stick it out here."

"I think they think they're special," Tom said. His voice was soft. It didn't have Mike's flamboyant, ironic edge. I felt a fluttering of apprehension.

"Yeah, but, dude, if you could get something for nothing, you'd do it. That's all they're doing. They can get away with it, because we give in to their demands. You can't really blame them," Mike said.

"Yeah, I guess. If I could get into school based on being white, then I would. But you don't see me trying to get something for nothing all the time like they do. It makes me sick."

A few days later, the students watched the scene in *The Color Purple* where Celie is beaten in the street by a white male character in the film.

"Well I'm depressed," Michelle said, as the lights came up. "Thanks Mrs. Reed, you're a real mood-killer!" That night, I read the students' journal entries about the book. They were supposed to write about the assigned reading, but Elizabeth emphasized that they were free to respond in any way that struck them—first impressions, questions, feelings, ideas. Mike usually found a way to fill up the word count requirement without saying anything. He was convinced Elizabeth didn't read the journals, even though she consistently called him on every instance of unrelated filler and graded him accordingly. One time he wrote all the words to the pledge of allegiance. Another time he wrote about how beautiful Elizabeth's long red hair was and then ended with a playful, "Now that will get me an A, won't it Mrs. Reed?" "No" she had written in the margin next to the question, and deducted points accordingly. For his entry on *The Color Purple*, Mike wrote about a transvestite who came into the restaurant Mike worked in: "It had long red nails and tried to talk in a high voice. It was wearing women's clothes. It ordered food and I didn't want to wait on it." Elizabeth wrote "lack of reflection or thought" at the top of the page and gave no points.

After the Spielberg scene, I noticed that he was quiet. I ventured a query: "What did you think?"

He shook his head. "White people suck. That's what I think."

The bell rang before I could press him for more. The students jumped as if there were springs in their chairs, grabbing bags and books and heading into the flow of bodies already swelling in the hallway outside the door.

A project like this one necessarily blends literacy ethnography, rhetorical analysis, ideological critique, and narrative. This blending helps in understanding a dynamic that Kathleen Blee (1992), in her study of the Ku Klux Klan, articulates in the following way: how divisive and destructive values like racism attract and persuade ordinary people, how and why individuals invest discursively in particular social positions, and how they might be persuaded to change. The notion of social change that animates this book has been central to composition studies for many years now. The possibility that exposure to new ideas or dialogue with others or critiques of privilege and injustice will lead students to develop rhetorical stances that promote rather than hinder racial justice—that such teaching will lead, eventually, to a more just, equitable society—these hopes have saturated research and writing in literacy studies and composition studies throughout my professional life. Two concepts, it seemed to me, as I finished analyzing the materials I collected during my year at Laurel Canyons, undergird this hope for social change: emotion in the context of persuasion—getting students to *feel* differently—and time—learning how and when and why racism originates and how its meanings shift across time and contexts, learning where it begins so that we can understand finally how to end it. I chose the title of this chapter, "Racism in Real Time," to emphasize the constraints of our concepts of narrative, pedagogical, and ethnographic time, and to show how these constraints limit our understanding of students like Mike and his racism. We tend to analyze such students one moment at a time. A colleague calls this the "gotcha!" mode of analysis in whiteness studies, where the goal is to expose isolated fragments of racist discourse. In this mode, we fail to place student racism in larger contexts, and thus we fail to understand its meaning for students, as well as our own role in creating the dynamics that give racism its power. This book is my attempt to explore these dynamics. It is my attempt to remember, in Ruth Behar's (2003) words, that in every head, and perhaps every heart, is an entire world.

RACISM, PERSUASION, AND EMOTION
REFLECTIONS ON THEN AND NOW

Throughout my year in Elizabeth's classroom, I was captivated by the drama of her struggles to enact a critical pedagogy in a public school that served a conservative, homogenous community. Daily I learned from Elizabeth the complexities involved in these struggles, which mirrored my own as a like-minded college professor but were different too. The difficulties in both cases often involved resistance by white students to antiracism or to multicultural lessons that critiqued racism, but I also came to see important differences: while I saw white student resistance as a theoretical and philosophical problem, in terms of not only the ethical issues of power and politics in writing classrooms but also the larger ideological forces of privilege and racism that seemed to influence white students, Elizabeth intuitively framed the challenges such students presented in both institutional and affective terms—as a problem at once circumscribed by school boards and required curricula, learning outcomes and relations with parents, and constrained by individual students' emotional development and feelings. Elizabeth's intuitive framing has become the backbone of the analysis I offer throughout this book.

In this chapter, I define some of the concepts—racism, persuasion, emotion—that are integral to the arguments I make in later chapters. In doing so, I create a framework for understanding racism in Elizabeth's terms—in terms, that is, of emotion and schooling. At the same time, I provide a kind of personal intellectual history of the roots of this project: how I became interested in questions of white students and racism in the context of literacy education, and how my understanding of these questions shifted throughout my research at Laurel Canyons.

A View of Race and Racism

When I began this research, the racial designation *white* was a relatively straightforward, even easy term for me. It was a term students in my own classrooms and at Laurel Canyons seemed to employ without self-consciousness as they described their own racial identities. It was a term that corresponded with official data about Laurel Canyons students posted on the district's Web site. It was also, of course, a term that named a body of research on antiracist education and sociological studies of race—Ruth Frankenberg's work on white women (1993), Matt Wray and Annalee Newitz's analyses of working-class white culture (1996), the essays collected in Richard Delgado and Jean Stefanic's anthology, *Critical White Studies: Looking behind the Mirror* (1997)—that were important to me as I formed my research questions. But as I began to analyze the materials I collected at Laurel Canyons, the term *white* became less self-evident. I began to see how students' voices and stories, their writing and responses to texts, complicated the representations of whiteness I found in the literature on antiracist education, where white students are often portrayed as tangled in structures of privilege and as therefore unable or unwilling to engage in critiques of racism or inequality. I began to see how much demographic data was hidden beneath the term with respect to not just social class but also peer group formation in school, the types of college that students aspired to, the different ways they experienced difference—on a church-sponsored trip to Jamaica, through an aunt who had married a person of color, via a brother who developed frightening neo-Nazi views on race. I also began to see what John Hartigan (1999) and Pamela Perry (2002) show in their ethnographies of white communities: white identity is formed in relation to other groups of whites as often as it is in relation to racial "others." In short, as my research at Laurel Canyons progressed, I began to notice how much ideological diversity and complexity lurked within white students, including those who regularly uttered offensive discourses about race.

Similarly, when I began this research, *racism* was a transparent term. Because I was interested in rhetoric and persuasion, I limited my definition of racism to language: discourses that promoted negative stereotypes of non-white groups, portrayed whites as more "normal" than or superior to other groups, denied claims of racism, denied that racism was a current social problem worthy of attention, blamed the victim for racism, characterized racism as a thing of the past or as something only "extreme" people believed in, creatively reinterpreted critiques of racism, promoted color-blindness ("we're all the same inside," "everybody's experienced oppression in one form or another"), or positioned whites as the victims of racism or of non-white people. Using the tools of critical discourse analysis, I found racist discourses in a number of the transcripts of class discussions, interviews, and copies of student writing that I generated during this study.

The racism, so defined, that I uncovered at Laurel Canyons, like the racism I have written about in other research projects, was sometimes subtle, hidden in well-intentioned but naïve understandings of racism and in student writers' struggles with new ideas and challenging academic tasks. It was sometimes overt, when white students openly rejected texts by people of color or asserted that whites are the victims of racial injustice. And it often existed in more ambiguous places, somewhere in between good intentions, naïveté, and racist belief, as white students searched for explanations of race that integrated the ideas they were encountering in class with their previous experiences and knowledge of the social world. This racism was familiar to me from my own teaching and from my experiences growing up in small all-white towns throughout the Midwest, though it has never lost its power to startle me. "You can't say Rodney King was beaten because he was Black," I remember a white student in one of my own classes announcing a few years ago, during a discussion of Anna Deavere Smith's *Twilight*, a drama about the Los Angeles riots. "White people get harassed by the cops all the time. They just don't complain about it as much, so you don't hear about it." I have been collecting such examples of racism from my classrooms for years now. And I've had countless conversations over the years with colleagues about problematic white student racism. I remember sitting just outside the mailroom in my department one day, reading a white student's essay that an outraged colleague had handed to me. The essay argued that African Americans should be grateful for slavery, because it rescued them from Africa and brought them to the United States.

As Joe Feagin and Debra Van Ausdale (2002) document, such racist beliefs continue seemingly unabated in the U.S.:

> Today, many white adults openly argue that racism targeting African Americans and other Americans of color is no longer a major problem central to U.S. society. . . . Indeed, many Whites couple this broad societal view with the related assertion that "I am not a racist," often while they assert in the next moment some negative view about racial "others." Today, the majority of white Americans seem to be in denial about the seriousness of racial prejudices, emotions, and discrimination in their own lives, the lives of their friends and relatives, and the larger society. . . . Racial discrimination and segregation are still central organizing factors in contemporary U.S. society. . . . For the most part, Whites and Blacks do not live in the same neighborhoods, attend the same schools at all educational levels, enter into close friendships or other intimate relationships with one another. . . . An Anti-Defamation League (1993) survey asked white respondents to evaluate eight anti-Black stereotypes, including such items as Black Americans "prefer to accept welfare" and have "less native intelligence." Three quarters of Whites agreed with one

or more of these stereotypes, with more than half agreeing with two or more. (28–30)

These anecdotes and the research on whiteness and racism that has emerged in the last several years suggest provocative relationships among privilege, whiteness, and racism. But they also raise hard and as-yet-unanswered questions: What do racist discourses mean to white students? Why do they find them persuasive? More pressingly, what can or should be done? As classroom teachers know and as much research suggests, attempting to teach white students to view race differently by asking them to read and write about race is often ineffective in combating such problems and sometimes even inadvertently fuels racist sentiments in white students. For example, Charles Gallagher's (1995) research has shown that efforts to engage white students in discussions of racial injustice actually motivate white students to solidify and fortify their identities as whites, encouraging them to view whites as under attack and to construct white victim narratives that compete with what they perceive to be claims of victimhood on the part of people of color. Beverly Tatum (1994) writes that reading about people of color often makes whites defensive and fails to provide them with alternative models of white racial identity rooted in social justice goals. More recent efforts to help white students interrogate their own racial identities (see McIntyre 1997; Wildman and Davis 2002; Winans 2005) have met with similar resistance or, perhaps even more problematically, have risked trading one label for another, focusing attention away from white privilege and toward poor and working-class whites, resulting in a game of "we're just as oppressed as other minority groups," as Jennifer Beech has pointed out (2004, 179).

In teacher education, efforts to teach whites about race have not fared much better. In Alice McIntyre's (1997) research with preservice teachers, "Making Meaning of Whiteness: Exploring Racial Identity with White Teachers," she critically analyzed the discourses employed by several white preservice teachers in her class as they explored racial identity. Her study aimed at "disrupting and eliminating the oppressive nature of whiteness . . . to examine complicity in racist talk and actions." McIntyre labels the discourses that she found to uphold racism as "white talk"—"[t]alk that serves to insulate white people from examination of their/our individual and collective roles in the perpetuation of racism." White talk, in McIntyre's study, replicates white structural advantage through discursive practices. Several subsequent studies of white discourse have come to a similar conclusion. Cynthia Lewis, Jean Ketter, and Bettina Fabos's "Reading Race in a Rural Context" (2001), an ethnographic case study of white teachers in a small midwestern town, argues that white participants were implicated in sustaining particular norms of whiteness even as they attempted to disrupt those norms. Kathy Hytten and John Warren's "Engaging Whiteness: How Racial Power Gets Reified in Education" (2003) emphasizes that racism derives from uncritical acceptance of racial privilege and an often unconscious desire to protect it. In their study of white preservice teachers, Hytten and Warren examined how white students engage in the "discourse of whiteness" even as they read and discuss whiteness as a topic of study. They describe how common, widely available discourses were used to inscribe whiteness and reify it in educational practice, and they note that white talk insulates participants from having to confront racial hierarchies or to examine how they benefit from them. Reviewing these and other studies, Sherry Marx (2003) grimly concludes that enlightening discussions of privilege and whiteness in the classroom do not necessarily lead to antiracism beyond it.

Other analyses of white identity, like Perry's (2002) study of racial identity in two high schools, Hartigan's (1999) ethnography of white communities in Detroit, and Newitz and Wray's (1996) explorations of the meaning of "white trash" were instrumental to me as I struggled to understand the relationship between whiteness and racism. These studies focused on the relationship between whiteness and social class identity, noting how class stratification creates racism and how racism helps justify and rationalize both class privilege and white class disenfranchisement. Hartigan and Perry insist that we need to understand socioeconomic subcommunities within broad labels like "white" and that such communities derive their sense of racial identity as much from each other as they do from groups of racialized others.

Indeed, as I listened to students at Laurel Canyons, I heard many connections between class and race and was often tempted to explain the racism I uncovered at the school by way of class analysis; moments when Mike compares the wealth of whites and Blacks, for example, or when Tom rationalizes racial injustice by way of middle-class-inflected discourses of hard work and individualism seem ripe with the significations of socioeconomic, class-based racism. But such analyses also have the potential to blind us to the rhetorical and emotioned processes at work in such moments, and they leave us with a pedagogical approach—exploring white privilege with students—that, as I'll argue in upcoming chapters, may be as ineffective as more traditional multicultural efforts focusing on raced and classed others.

In the end, I found that collecting examples of racism and reading about others' efforts at such collection—identifying, naming, labeling, and analyzing forms of racist talk in students—was a fascinating but ultimately somewhat fruitless exercise. The examples suggested only more questions. It wasn't until I began to see racism in rhetorical and emotioned terms, rather than simply as a political phenomenon, that I began to get at the questions that most interested me: Why were students persuaded by racism? How could they be persuaded differently?

A View of Race and Racism in Terms of Persuasion and Emotion

To answer these questions, I began to situate my analysis of racism within broader research on what Ellen Quandahl, quoting Lynn Worsham, calls "pedagogy as paideia, the whole social education of members of a culture" (11). Part of understanding paideia, Quandahl writes, entails attention to emotion as not merely an individual or natural phenomenon but also part of culture and history, closely linked to rhetoric and to schooling. Paideia "address[es] humans in ways that shape what is said to be deeply 'within,' offering not only knowledge, perspective, and strategies of reason, but also the very forms of emotion" (Quandahl, 11).

How schooling addresses students in ways that are "deeply within" and the effects of this aspect of schooling in terms of students' attitudes and beliefs about race began to replace the focus on collecting and analyzing forms of racism with which I began my research. Instead, at Laurel Canyons, I began to trace racist discourses to their roots in sometimes counterintuitive and often nonracist places. I began to pay attention not only to instances of racism but also to the emotions that gave rise to them and to the ways those emotions were taught to—even demanded of—students in school. As Brian Massumi writes, we have as yet no cultural-theoretical vocabulary specific to emotion or affect. Without such a vocabulary, it is all too easy for "received psychological categories to slip back in" (1996, p. 221). And as Srivastata (2005) writes, "there have been few sustained observations of how and why" emotional responses "block, diffuse, and distract from change" in "pedagogical sites" (1). In this sense, my study of race at Laurel Canyons draws from and contributes to the critical study of emotions, what Jenny Edbauer Rice calls the "interdisciplinary study of affect and its mediating force in everyday life (201–2)." I follow Ann Cvetkovich in an effort to "forge methodologies for the documentation and examination of the structures of affect that constitute cultural experience and serve as the foundation for public cultures" (11).

As Megan Boler (1999) writes, our emotional experiences inform both our cognitive and our moral perceptions. "Our emotions help us to envision future horizons of possibilities and who we want to become" (xviii). Because education teaches social and moral values, education is inextricably tied to emotional control (Boler). Emotional control occurs through taken-for-granted practices, what Daniel Gross (2006) calls "technologies of emotion" (4). As Gross writes, the contours of our emotional world have been shaped by institutions: Emotions such as anger presume a public stage, and our most powerful emotional responses are constituted in the social world (2). Lindquist (2004) similarly suggests that as teachers we need a much richer understanding of "how affective dimensions . . . participate in the development of actionable beliefs" (191). These and other scholars working on the role of emotion in learning and in ideological processes have made clear that emotions are central to how we process our political beliefs and formulate rational understandings of the social world (see, for example, Jacobs and Micciche 2003).

Recent scholarship on the critical study of emotion—embodied in such diverse texts as Massumi's *Parables for the Virtual: Movement, Affect, Sensation* (2002); Jack Barbalet's *Emotions, Social Theory, and Social Structure* (1998); Boler's *Feeling Power: Emotions and Education"* (1999); Lila Abu-Lughod and Catherine Lutz's *Language and the Politics of Emotion* (1990); and Gross's *The Secret History of Emotion* (2006), to name a few—makes clear the following:

1. Emotions cannot be seen as distinct from reason. Emotions are intertwined with rational decision making and are central to the construction of belief. As Laura Micciche (2003) notes, "emotion is a central ingredient in the act of persuasion . . . [and must be viewed] as connected to our rational and ethical lives" (3, 5).

2. Emotions are not private, individual experiences; they are socially experienced and constructed. Their construction takes place through language, and thus, as Michalinos Zembylas writes, "emotion is a *discursive practice*" (2005, 937, italics original). Emotion acquires its "meaning and force from its location and performance in the public realm of discourse" (Abu-Lughod and Lutz 1990, 7). Emotion is central to the study of rhetoric and to understanding rhetorical processes.

3. Emotion is taught and learned at home and at school. It is an important, deeply embedded site of social control. Boler writes that "the social control of emotions is a central and underexplored aspect of education in relation to hegemony" (4). Contradictory rules about emotion and its expression uphold the dominant culture's hierarchies and values (xvii). We are taught how to feel as part of our socialization into a particular culture's dominant norms.

If, at the beginning of this project, my overriding questions were about the persuasive power of racism, research on emotion has helped me formulate the following powerfully related subquestions:

> What emotioned rules were taught at Laurel Canyons, and how were they taught?

How and when were emotioned rules performed and enacted? How
were they applied and policed across situations and contexts?

How did emotioned learning participate in the development of racial
identity and in the construction of persuasive discourses about
race?

Consequently, I began to pay attention not just to students' racist utterances but also to the emotioned rules that surrounded them. I defined
emotioned rules as implicit norms of behavior, attitude, intellectual habits,
values, and practices that were taught and enforced via emotional exhortation in school (when students were encouraged to feel a particular way—to
avoid anger, for example—in order to achieve a certain behavioral, academic, intellectual, or moral outcome such as the avoidance of social conflict or
loss of classroom control). In focusing on emotioned rules, I am following in
a tradition of sociology that has seen social, linguistic, and emotional rules
as central to understanding how social life is reproduced (Goffman 1967,
1969; Hochschild 1979) and that has understood emotional control to be an
important arena of study (Hochschild, 1979). But I am also deviating from
this model in my focus on the relationship between systems of emotioned
rules and processes of persuasion, in particular, the connections between
specific emotioned rules at Laurel Canyons and the persuasive power of
commonly asserted racist discourses.

Crowley's (2006) analysis of the emotioned dimensions of rhetorical processes provides a way of understanding these connections. Citing research in
cognitive psychology, Crowley explains the principle of elaboration, which
posits that "'the extent of affective influence depends on whether the experience is elaborated or punctuated, and the potential for elaboration depends
on the structure of beliefs regarding the object of attribution'" (Crowley,
84). "An elaborated experience is one that is connected to other experiences
and memories of such encounters; a punctuated experience is not so connected" (Crowley, 85). When a particular racist discourse is connected, via
emotioned rules taught in school, to other sites of learning and to other
pedagogical and institutional contexts, this discourse becomes "elaborated"
for students. This connection, or elaboration, helps explain the persuasive
pull of the discourse.

Reading racism at Laurel Canyons through the lens provided by scholarship on emotion yielded a very different interpretation of what racism is
and where it comes from. I began to see that the persuasive power of racist
discourses cannot be explained by what is generally understood as "racism"—that is, negative attitudes or feelings toward nonwhite people arising
from ignorance, lack of empathy, or a desire to maintain race privileges.

Because the power of racism lies elsewhere, students will not be persuaded by many current antiracist pedagogical practices that aim to rectify problems of ignorance or privilege, including multicultural literacy and attempts to make "whiteness" the subject of classroom inquiry and critique. Attention to the underlying affective resonances of racist discourses makes clear that although such talk often promotes racism, racism as we've understood it—as either a response born of ignorance or a latent desire to protect white privilege—does not explain its meaning or appeal.

Paradoxically, the language of racism—particularly those familiar, widely available, and deeply offensive discourses ("my ancestors didn't own slaves"; "[people of color] could make it if they would try harder")—is rarely a straightforward reflection of racial hostility, prejudice, or a desire to protect privilege. Instead it often expresses a host of latent emotions unrelated to race per se. To understand this paradox, it is important to examine the multiple, contradictory levels on which forms of talk about race attract students and to unpack the symbolic and metaphoric coherence of this talk for students, for whom such talk has multiple and varied meanings, not always reducible to a particular racial politics. In fact, the symbolic coherence of talk about race is obscured when we view it solely in terms of its political effects, as methodologies such as critical discourse analysis tend to encourage (Gee 1992; Fairclough and Wodak 1997). Racist discourses express a wide array of meanings, collapsing them into the reductive clarity of familiar rhetorical forms—"Blacks complain more than whites"; "white people can't get jobs because of affirmative action." Such talk maps a dialectic between the affective and associative dimensions of language and the racial politics such speech forwards. A single idea—reverse racism, whites as victims, color blindness, white innocence—compresses a multitude of meanings that are not reducible to racial self-interest, racial identity, or racist belief. This analysis helped me see that the difficulties educators often report in their attempts to teach white students about race stem from a failure to understand these underlying meanings, to miss the persuasive coherence of talk about race, and thus to misunderstand what kinds of pedagogical interventions might lead to change. I began to see, for example, that in my own classrooms, I had focused too narrowly on the political meanings of such discourses—on the ways white students promote racism in their speech—rather than on the individual subjective coherence and symbolic, affective associations that racist discourse, like all individually and culturally persuasive discourse, provides for students.

For example, in my research (Trainor 2001 and 2005), students have explained that the claim that their ancestors were innocent of racism was a way of connecting with people of color, a way of expressing, for them, racial solidarity, by suggesting that they were on the "right" side of struggles over racial justice. Seen in this light, the claim that "my ancestors didn't own slaves" taps a world where differences between oppressor and oppressed groups are eradicated by the claims of family. "My ancestors," this discourse said to white students, "were on your side." Of course, this discourse is problematic: it erases the ways race gave rise to very real material, political, and social differences in the United States. (In this sense, white ancestors and slave ancestors are decidedly not "on the same side.") But it is important to see, as well, the emotional appeals embedded in this discourse, its promise of solidarity through kinship and across history, and the desire for racial fellowship it expresses. The student who asserts that his ancestors were innocent of racism is not only forwarding a racial politics that exonerates whites from responsibility. He is also expressing a host of desires for racial understanding and healing; "my ancestors never owned slaves" taps these feelings and expresses them in a concise, powerful, and thus persuasive way. Understanding both the political *and* private dimensions of such utterances, as well as the institutional context that gives them force (as I'll suggest in the next section), is one key to understanding why such utterances persuade students and thus to figuring out how teachers committed to antiracism can create multicultural and antiracist curricula that persuade them differently.

A View of Racism in the Context of School

My first indication that school had something to do with the emotions that make some racist discourses—such as "my ancestors didn't own slaves"—persuasive came at a moment, early in the fall of my year at Laurel Canyons, when I perceived a connection between the bright yellow smiley-face beanbag sitting prominently near the bookshelves in Elizabeth's classroom, the student aide who added "Have a great day!" at the end of the pledge of allegiance as she recited it over the loudspeaker each morning, and students' rejection of Maya Angelou as "whiny" and "complaining too much." In attempting to articulate the connections between such seemingly disparate elements, I began to realize that students' rejection of Angelou wasn't about race. It stemmed from a sense of unfairness: students weren't allowed to complain in or about school—they were exhorted constantly to "look on the bright side" and "focus on the positive," to "have a great day," even when they had reasons for their discontent—so why was Angelou allowed to write "a book about complaining," to use one student's words?

Thus did I come to the second part of my argument about racism: in the same way that schools function as a site of social class disciplining (Boler 1999; Larabee 1997), they also provide "race disciplining"; that is, they teach the emotioned frames within which racist discourses become persuasive. Taken-for-granted and tacit school practices and values often set up rhetorical and affective frames that inadvertently scaffold racist discourse. These tacit practices and values function as "emotioned rules," and in my research I began to ask what rules are taught, how they are enacted and enforced, and most important, how they participate in the development of beliefs about race that are persuasive to students.

Though schools clearly do not "teach" racial identity in the way they teach multiplication or punctuation, schools are settings where people acquire some version "of the rules of racial classification" and of their own racial identity (Lewis 2004, 4). In educational research, as Lewis argues, we have not understood that students learn what race means for themselves and others in the context of everyday interaction in school. For example, at Laurel Canyons, teachers, coaches, and administrators emphasized to students the importance of a positive attitude in sports, social life, and academic endeavors. As a result, students often told each other to "keep a good attitude" and they often interpreted literature so that it too taught the power of positive thinking. When they read Angelou's *I Know Why the Caged Bird Sings*, they praised Angelou for her positive attitude and condemned those passages in the book where Angelou critiques racism. Students felt that in those passages, Angelou was overly negative, and thus they dismissed her claims about racism as "whiny." But this dismissal of her claims about racism, problematic though it was, was rooted in a critique of her perceived negativity rather than in racist feelings per se, and this critique emerged from values and attitudes that were learned and taught in school. In this way, Laurel Canyons promoted troubling racist discourses, even as it worked overtly to combat racism.

As I began to unpack this insight, my attention turned to research on the hidden curriculum. Indeed, educators have long said that schools function as sites of social class disciplining, and they have long pointed to the effects of the "hidden curriculum" in providing this disciplining. The hidden curriculum refers to invisible school practices that are expressed in the school environment: in classroom climate, furniture arrangement, pedagogical methods, teacher-student interactions, student-to-student interactions, and many other invisible or taken-for-granted dynamics (Schugurensky 2002, 3). For example, the hidden curriculum of high schools provides, as David Larabee (1997) writes, a "competitive arena, an incentive for individual striving, or a . . . merit-based reward structure" (98) that legitimates capitalist social and economic arrangements. In high schools, Larabee argues, some of the most important elements of bourgeois ideology are learned, practiced, and legitimized (98). Another evocation of the hidden curriculum, Lynn Bloom's (1996) "Freshman Composition as a Middle-Class Enterprise," extends this analysis to the college writing classroom. Bloom lists several middle-class virtues—self-reliance, respectability, decorum, thrift, order, efficiency, cleanliness, punctuality, delayed gratification—that are reinforced by common practices of college literacy education.

But the hidden curriculum as a heuristic is incomplete in a number of ways. It is overly deterministic, for example, and doesn't allow a way to see how individuals make use of the material the curriculum provides. Nicole DeVoss, Ellen Cushman, and Jeffrey Grabill's (2005) notion of infrastructure provides a way of bringing the heuristic power of the hidden curriculum to bear on the workings of racism in school without the reproductive determinism of some analyses of the hidden curriculum and social class. As DeVoss, Cushman, and Grabill articulate it, infrastructures have several features: they are "embedded," or sunk into and inside, other structures, social arrangements, and technologies; they are both spatial and temporal, and their scope or effect reaches beyond a single event or one-site practice; they are learned as part of membership, and knowledge of their organizational arrangements and artifacts is "a *sine qua non* of membership in a community of practice" (20); they are linked with other conventions of practice; they are built on an installed base and "wrestle with the inertia" of that base, inheriting its strengths and limitations.

Infrastructure helps us understand several aspects of the hidden curriculum: it suggests that the hidden curriculum is a shifting rather than a static set of implicit lessons, in that infrastructure is shaped by and shapes conventions of practice. It suggests that the hidden curriculum is an embedded phenomenon and that its various parts are built into and connected to one another, that new pedagogical practices and changing social relations must "wrestle with the inertia of the installed base" to become part of the infrastructure (DeVoss, Cushman, and Grabill, 21). It suggests that infrastructure reaches beyond its immediate physical or temporal enactment to influence practice beyond a single event or practice, that practices are related—metaphorically, linguistically—to each other.

Just as important, DeVoss, Cushman, and Grabill also note that there is more to an infrastructure than what is material or technological: "[Infrastructure] includes standards and classifications—most powerfully what counts as writing, what is permissible in a writing class, and what makes for "good" writing. Infrastructure also entails decision-making processes and the values and power relationships enacted by those processes, and infrastructure is thoroughly penetrated by issues of culture and identity" (22). If the hidden curriculum, as a heuristic, allowed us to see how schools legitimized and internalized structures of social class difference and inequity but did so in a static, deterministic way, "infrastructure" as a heuristic allows us to get at other ideological processes—like the legitimization and internalization of particular ideologies of race—and to do so in a way that highlights the psychosocial and rhetorical dynamics of improvisation, unpredictability, and idiosyncrasy that characterize any social process. Throughout the following chapters, I note the ways that infrastructural elements at Laurel Canyons supported, taught, or insisted on particular emotioned rules, and I look at how the enactment of these rules in turn supported racism.

A View of Pedagogical, Ethnographic, and Narrative Time

Quandahl (2003) suggests that "deliberate emotional education" ought to include "deep thought about how institutions teach and manage emotion, and broad opportunities to learn and reflect on what happens when people feel in certain situations" (20). "Deep thought" on how institutions manage emotions takes us to questions about how the hidden and tacit aspects of our pedagogy inadvertently teach emotional dispositions that run contrary to the more explicit political and rhetorical work we are trying to accomplish. Such questions should include the following: What emotioned rules do we teach, intentionally or not, and what political projects do those rules, again intentionally or not, support? How can we begin to teach different emotioned rules? Can we make our own performances of emotioned positions—our commitment to justice, for example; our enthusiasm for difference and complexity—more salient so that they might serve as alternative models for students? How can we make space for what Lindquist calls "students' emotional labor in scenes of literacy learning" (189)? These questions make clear that moving white students toward antiracism will require more than rational argument about injustice or privilege, or exposure to racial others in classroom texts. We might think instead of students' manifestation of racism as the final performance of a persuasive process like that articulated by Kenneth Burke, where persuasion takes place not through "one particular address, but [through] a general body of identifications that owe their convincingness much more to trivial repetition and dull daily reinforcement than to rhetorical skill" (26). This persuasive process acquires its force simultaneously from the institutional and social practices of daily life in school and from the realm of emotions that is both constructed by and responsive to those practices. It is an understanding of persuasion that is echoed in Lynn Worsham's evocative definition of emotion as "the tight braid of affect and judgment, socially and historically constructed and bodily lived, through which the symbolic takes hold of and binds the individual to the social order" (1998, 216).

This articulation of how schools scaffold emotioned rules and how these rules interact with available discourses about race to make particular racial ideologies persuasive necessitates a rhetorical, rather than a developmental or sequential, model of racial learning. In the field of composition in particular, scholars have emphasized a need for antiracist teachers to work rhetorically (Anderson 1997), a view supported by my research at Laurel Canyons. A rhetorical view of learning differs significantly from more commonly held developmental models. In developmental models, persuading a student to see race differently requires an intervention in the student's consciousness, something that it is hoped can be achieved by a sequenced series of exposures to difference and to new ideas. But this model overlooks a crucial aspect of the process of persuasion: what Lindquist (2002) calls the public dimension of persuasion, how ideas get taken up, changed, and incorporated into social groups, recursively, over time.

Chronology and time became important to me for a number of reasons as I thought about the students at Laurel Canyons and about the notions of race and persuasion at the center of this book. In *Culture and Truth: The Remaking of Social Analysis* (1993), Renato Rosaldo reflects on ethnographic treatments of time, noting that field-workers often contrast the "time-discipline" of Western cultures with its perceived opposite in the field, where natives live without the segmentation and structuring of time that mark life in industrialized societies. But rather than seeing time structure as absent, Rosaldo proposes trying to characterize what he calls the "tempo of social life," which for him is a source of indeterminacy—of "optionality, variability, and unpredictability" (112). Schools, perhaps more than any other institution in modern Western cultures, embody the kind of time-discipline that ethnographers have contrasted with traditional societies. As many have pointed out, the school calendar, from August to May, is strictly followed even though the circumstances of its original intent—to allow the children of farmers to return home to help with planting, cultivation, and harvest—have long passed. Subject matter is divided into timed segments, signaled by bells. Students themselves are classified by their ages and the numbers of years they have spent in school. Course materials are sequenced so that concepts, ideas, and skills build on each other, allowing students to gain and demonstrate mastery by a particular point in time. Race, like other forms of learning, is often understood by teachers and educators in time-saturated ways. When I talk to people about my research on students and racism, particularly when I give an example of a problematic response to a multicultural text, one common reaction is to suggest that in time, such responses will give way to more mature (less racist) thinking. But I am not interested in tracing how, over time, racist ideas mutate into more nuanced understandings (nor am I convinced that time will work its magic in quite this way). This is not a success story in that sense, where the reader witnesses a savvy teacher and a smart curriculum that promote antiracism and growth over time. Rather it is the story that attempts to capture "the tempo of social being" (Rosaldo 1993, 11), a concept of time that does not reduce to concepts of segmentation and sequencing, to closure, or what Raymond Williams (1977) calls "fixed forms." This concept of time is a source of indeterminacy: it complicates the growth narratives that undergird most school-based concepts of time, where students will learn, over time, to become less racist, for example. It suggests instead that the messy social tempo of life in school may sometimes work to structure learning in the opposite direction, or in directions not discernible to us. Elizabeth Ellsworth calls this the "impossibility" of teaching—the ways in which learning in real time unfolds outside of our pedagogical control.

Attention to the tempo of social interaction and to the unpredictability and nonlinear nature of students' ideas about race requires a rhetorical engagement with narratives and narrative time. Writing narrative helped me reconcile the tension between the stasis of "fixed forms"—the ethnographic remnants and records of what people said and did and wrote, all of which exist only in the moment of writing, in the one-dimensional realms of field notes and transcripts—and the dynamism of the research itself, the lively living presence of the people involved in the project. It helped me move past the "gotcha!" mode of analysis, where a moment of student racism is isolated in a transcript and represented ethnographically in a way that is divorced from other moments in time. That narratives offer such promise to ethnographers is not a new idea: There is a long history of narrative studies in the social sciences, where an interest in rhetoric and storytelling has accompanied a shift toward viewing ethnography as interpretive and textual, more humanities than science. As Deborah Hicks (2002) writes, narrative functions as a "mode of thought and a means of constructing knowledge . . . a means of engaging students and teachers in critical reflection . . . and through which students construe identities and construct moral selves" (137). For Hicks, the classic educational narrative of this sort is Mike Rose's (1990) *Lives on the Boundary*, a hybrid text that weaves between autobiography, narrative, and argument: "Rich details about literacies and lives are revealing of the desires and search for belonging so integral to Rose's learning experiences and to his later readings and rhetorical shapings of other 'lives on the boundary.' The reader is not distanced from feeling and moral complexity; the more generalized arguments that frame the text emerge in close dialogue with such particulars" (Hicks 2002, 140).

Drawing in particular on Lila Abu-Lughod's (1993) and Deborah Britzman's (2006) explorations of the relationships between fiction, representation, ethnography, and emotion, I employ narrative as a way to remind readers that research can be conceptualized as "a thought experiment, a note of counter-discourse" (Britzman, ix), something closer to a novelist's truth. As Britzman asks, rhetorically, if we claim we are writing novels, must that cancel the question of truth (viii)? Ethnographic attention to the power and pull of narrative means an engagement with the process of creating stories and with their epistemological consequences. This engagement is particularly important in an ethnographic account of race, where overdetermined narratives, characters, and plots already abound. To open up those meanings to further scrutiny, I played with order and sequence throughout the book, in its overall organization (chronological) and in its emphasis on originating points, motives, and causes. I also played with time by juxtaposing moments rendered in different genres: at times I employ the narrative techniques of creative nonfiction; at other times I give large chunks of text over to students' stories told in their own voices. I also use the traditional techniques of ethnographic representation, looking at social dynamics up close, in transcript form.

In analyzing the transcripts, I pay attention to interconnected themes that link ideas about race across other school and social contexts in ways that may seem counterintuitive. My aim here is to trace the dynamics of race talk to other social, institutional, and private dynamics, showing how, in Blee's (1992) formulation, race "attracts ordinary people into its politics" (4). The transcripts highlight a central argument of the book, that attention to the underlying resonances—affective, associative, metaphoric—of talk about race makes clear that although such talk often promotes racism, racism per se hardly begins to explain its meaning or appeal, and that to understand its appeal, we need to look at school itself. In this sense, ethnographic analysis undergirds narrative representation, as I show how discourses originate in constellations of feeling often taught in school, get taken up in particular contexts, often with racist effect. Research on race has often begun at the ending in this sense, by examining the political meanings of racist language rather than seeing politics as an ending point, the result of a complex ambulatory route across feeling, social dynamic, and institutional contexts. Rather than moving forward from a problematic student paper or a problematic utterance in class, unpacking its political ramifications in terms of race and embarking on attempts to teach the student differently, I am interested in moving backward in time and in focus, paying attention to multiple levels: the idiosyncratic, associative meanings of race for students and the institutional, cultural, and social dynamics that gave talk about race its persuasive force in the first place. Narrative and chronology have been central to this effort.

So have questions of representation, as I have struggled with drawing compassionate, respectful portraits of students without losing sight of the racism they often promoted. Walking this tightrope involves what Krista

Ratcliffe calls "rhetorical listening," which she defines as a "trope for interpretive invention" and "a code of cross-cultural conduct." Such listening signifies "a stance of openness that a person may choose to assume in relation to any person, text, or culture" (1), and it requires identification through commonalities and differences. Case in point: Laurel Canyons students have had virtually no social interactions with people of color in their communities or school. Facts like these surprised me when I began my research at Laurel Canyons. The students seemed so isolated, so sheltered and naïve. But I also remember my own history, growing up in all-white, all-Christian towns throughout the Midwest. Like many of the students in this study, I grew up without ever having had sustained social interactions with people of color. In the recently desegregated southern Texas public school where I spent my first-, second-, and third-grade years, African American children sat on the opposite side of the classroom, which had been divided according to "ability": I sat with children who were deemed, by white teachers, as "good" readers and who were, not surprisingly, themselves all white. African American children sat on the other side of the classroom, on the remedial side. I remember listening to their voices, subdued, sometimes stumbling, as they sounded out words for the teacher. In the sixth grade, I lived in a small town in central Kansas. I remember that a boy from Vietnam transferred into my class for a few months before moving again. I remember that he didn't speak English and that he had a deep scar on his cheek. My first social interactions with people who were not white did not occur until I was twenty-five, teaching for the first time at a large public university. Among many strange and unsettling experiences that year, I remember reading a journal entry from one of my students, an African American woman much older than I was. She wrote that she didn't think white people could be effective teachers in multiracial classrooms. I took her point personally—as perhaps I was meant to—and felt a deep sense of unease and discomfort. Carefully well-intentioned beliefs about myself seemed to crumble around me. Sitting in the office I shared with other part-timers and graduate students, I wrote a lengthy rebuttal in the margins of the loose-leaf pages of my student's journal. I remember making scratches on a notepad, trying to get the words right. I even considered quoting some other, more convincing authority to buttress the argument I was making, and spent several minutes thumbing through the books on pedagogy and teaching that were scattered around the office. When I finished, I showed the journal and my response to one of my office mates, a seasoned teacher, also white. She read silently, then handed me a small bottle of correction fluid from her drawer. "Let's start over," she said. "White this out, and write over what you've written, something like "It sounds like you've had some tough experiences with this. I would like to hear more about it" and then leave it at that. Okay? You should leave it at that."

I remember this as a kind of beginning—a moment when I first saw the edges of a territory I hadn't known existed, a territory far wider and perhaps more enlivening than the world of racial ideas—"we're all the same inside," "skin color doesn't matter,"—that I had inhabited. There are other beginnings, of course, going both farther back and ahead in time. They are markers; they punctuate the formation of my racial awareness and consciousness. Williams (1977) writes, "The strongest barrier to the recognition of human cultural activity is this immediate and regular conversion of experience into finished products. . . . [It is misleading to habitually project endings] not only into the always moving substance of the past, but into contemporary life, in which relationships, institutions and formations in which we are still actively involved are converted, by this procedural mode, into formed wholes rather than forming and formative processes" (128–29). Williams's point, that we need to examine our conversions of the present into the past, is central to my work as an ethnographer and to my understanding of my research subjects' racial beliefs.

That I so readily recall my own racialized beginning stories both smoothes over and complicates many of the tensions that exist between me and the all-white participants in my study. Memories of my own racial formation and whiteness ensure that as a researcher at Laurel Canyons, I am not an outsider studying a group of people who appear to me as other. And yet my identity as a researcher and teacher with a commitment to antiracist pedagogies also separates me from the white students at Laurel Canyons and from the ways of talking about race that I am interested in studying. This separation is important to understand. First, my goal in this book is to understand talk about race as it occurred in Elizabeth's classroom, but I also have a broader goal: to understand racially divisive speech, racist discourse, and racist rhetorical forms. Because my primary concern is racism, racism naturally overshadows, throughout the book, many countervailing views. The students whose stories I focus on, for example, all espoused or acquiesced to racist points of view at several different points in the school year. In this way, they weren't actually exceptional: of the fifteen students I came to know over the course of the school year, ten fell into this category. I did not focus on students who consistently opposed racism. However, this isn't to say that the focal students were uniformly racist. To the contrary, they often made assertions about the importance of racial harmony and expressed confusion and dismay when confronted with evidence of continuing racism. But at other times, they made racist claims or nodded vigorously when a classmate made such claims. In this way, the students I focus on in upcoming chapters struggled for new and different understandings of race as they simultaneously insisted on points of view that reified racial hierarchies and stereotypes. I found their struggles compelling, which is partly why I chose them as focal students. The students who consistently made more complex, nuanced, tolerant claims about race also figure in the narratives I recount here, so these forms of talk about race are represented as well. But because of the goals of the book, their voices do not dominate.

One of the book's controlling questions is how particular notions of race come to matter to people and what role the cultural practices, rituals, and resources of literacy education play in that process. At Laurel Canyons, such questions were rarely explicitly addressed pedagogically or in the school's multicultural curricula. But categories of raced meanings were asserted, negotiated, revised, reincorporated, and reiterated at many levels of school culture, particularly at the level of interactions that took place around literacy. This circulation, shifting, and mutation within a classroom are matters of persuasion, a term I use in the rhetorical sense—convincing or enticing someone to adopt a particular point of view—to understand a process not typically considered rhetorically: the continuing pull and power of racist discourse in the United States. In one sense, persuasion might be understood as a dynamic that names how people become convinced or not of ideas promoted by others in their stories, testimonies, and arguments, how people change and make up their minds about the issues, questions, and dilemmas they confront in their worlds. This definition of persuasion shows an understanding of the dynamic between discourses and individuals as private—as something that happens in individuals to change the deep structure of belief (Lindquist 2002). But persuasion is also a public, social process, a matter of how "individuals examine their identities to determine what they are and how they fit into groups with others who share those identities" (Kenneth Burke quoted in Heath 1986, 202). As Lindquist writes, "to understand the particulars of persuasion for a given culture is to understand how that culture establishes itself *as* culture—how it invents and sustains its mythologies and what circumstances must obtain in order for these mythologies to change" (4).

Throughout my research, I was interested in the public notion of persuasion that Lindquist articulates—interested, that is, in how, over time, groups of people come to accept a point of view as true. This was one of the reasons I sought an all-white environment for the research: it would allow me to investigate the public, collective nature of racist discourses. But my understanding of the relationship between individual, or private, utterance and public, collective belief systems has grown more complex.

I have begun to see that the public dynamic of persuasion that Lindquist writes of cannot actually be separated from the more familiar notion of persuasion as a private, individual change of heart. This notion of persuasion as something private, in fact, undergirds a second part of my argument: the multiple and often contradictory paths by which individuals are attracted to an idea or become convinced of its truth. These paths cannot be reduced to unidimensional factors, such as a student's racial identity or position of privilege, his or her beliefs or values. Listening to the students at Laurel Canyons, for example, taught me that racist discourses are not always motivated by, and often cannot be traced to, racist sentiment or belief. Similarly, they cannot be traced to a person's position within the racial or class or gender hierarchies of our society. Talk about race instead persuaded by way of symbolic and metaphoric resonances that appealed on affective and associative levels and that could not be reduced to a particular racial politics. I have thus found it useful to treat race in rhetorical terms, separating it from inferences about a person's identity or beliefs. Such a move, paradoxically, allowed me to formulate a view of persuasion and race—a view of how language about race resonates with individuals, among social groups, and within institutional contexts—that understands the language of race in its multidimensionality as, on the one hand, the forwarding of particular racial politics that serves the interests of whites and, on the other, aspects of a constantly shifting shared social language that easily converts to a private realm of ideas, values, and beliefs often paradoxically unrelated to race per se.

When I began this research, I wanted to provide a description of the problem of white racism in the classroom that opened up new possibilities of interpretation. I didn't intend to offer prescriptions, solutions, or answers; nor was my goal to expose or indict. I was not interested in condemning students (or their teacher) for failing to "get" critical education or for espousing views that I found troubling and offensive. And at the same time, I didn't want to valorize students as repositories of resistant, alternative wisdom (though I did sometimes find such counterwisdom in what they said). I was determined to create an ethnographic form that would allow me to avoid demonizing students as hopelessly racist and ignorant, in need of transformative interventions. But at the same time, I wanted very much to illuminate the ways white students' everyday language reproduced and supported racial injustice. I wanted to follow Ellen Brantlinger (2003) when she writes that the goal of conducting research about people who appear to promote injustice is not to incriminate research participants for wrongdoing but to use their stories to illustrate the nature of social injustice in public institutions.

And yet the line between incrimination and illumination is so fine. Ironically, one of the last insights I gleaned from this research is also one of the most personal. This insight has to do with processes of representation and identity and ethnography. It is about what draws ethnographers to particular research sites and how they construct what they find there. When I began this research, Laurel Canyons students were other to me: they supported views I abhorred, they embodied values I renounced. While I still abhor racism, I've begun nonetheless to question these constructions. Virginia Anderson (2000) writes of the complexities of writing about those whose beliefs and values place them on the other side of the ethical boundaries we've drawn, who advocate positions that we feel ethically bound to challenge. Anderson's uneasy resolution of this dilemma is an injunction to social justice teachers to open themselves up to the "mystery" of such students. At the beginning of this research, I took Anderson's point very seriously. I saw my job as trying to understand students whose values and beliefs contradicted and opposed my own. I saw that this meant interrogating the whiteness I inhabit myself—a racial identity I can't erase but an identity, nevertheless, under a constant kind of self-revision. And I understood that my work was part of an attempt to, in Anderson's words, "accept rhetorical responsibility in our on-going persuasive encounters with students . . . [and] to open up to the mystery" (458) of ways of talking and believing about race that I find offensive, that fall on the other side of the lines I've drawn about race and justice. Anderson's point echoes Raymond Williams (1977) when he writes that "the first task of any social theory is . . . to analyze the forms which have determined certain (interpreted) inclusions and certain (categorical) exclusions" (149). But thinking about Williams now, I see the particulars. I see, for example, how one narrative of my journey through this research places me in a particular place in time, as the enlightened antiracist educator and researcher, trying to understand students who are racially like me but ideologically other. But another story, with a different chronology, farther back in time, might not show difference at all. In this version, my "character" doesn't see an other in Laurel Canyons students. Instead, she hears in these students' voices resonant, even compelling, echoes of her own small-town midwestern childhood. In this chronology, Laurel Canyons students aren't other at all; they are intensely, intimately familiar.

This familiarity—the sense of connection I felt at Laurel Canyons to students who are so ideologically different—is born of rhetorical listening in the service of ethnographic understanding, and as Ratcliffe predicts, it compels me to create a differently structured narrative, one where the self-other, researcher-researched lines are drawn more flexibly, with more nuance and care. Drawing such lines is no simple task: Racial inequality is real. People promote and benefit from it. I want to help end it. In the chapter that follows, I attempt to make Laurel Canyons students and their racist discourses familiar to readers as well, by telling the students' stories and chronicling the goings-on in their English classroom during the fall of the year in which I conducted the research. Such familiarity, I've learned, cuts in many ways. It opens up my own self-construction as a white person. It fosters critical self-reflection on whiteness and racism. It also makes it impossible to "other" students whose racism I nonetheless abhor and thus forces me to find new answers and explanations for it.

2

CLASS BEGINNINGS
SEPTEMBER AND OCTOBER

> A story is always situated; it has both a teller and an audi-
> ence. Its perspective is partial . . . and its telling is motivated.
> —L. Abu-Lughod, *Writing Women's Worlds: Bedouin Stories*

Beginnings

Laura described her first encounter with racism like this:

We went to my mom's family reunion. . . . We had driven four straight hours each way to get there. I remember this so well, the whole day. It really stands out to me. I remember my dad said, it's summer solstice, the hottest, longest day of the year. And I remember, I played with my cousins all day, in this big park with a pond you could swim in. I had such a good day. I was 11 years old, still young and innocent—ha! That didn't last long!

Because later that day, I heard my uncles and two of my cousins who were, you know, already grown up, and one of my uncles used the "n" word, a lot. He was talking about Black people and how they sponge off people and how much he just, hated them, I guess. I heard everything he said. It was the first time I saw racism. I had never heard anyone talk like that, and I kept hearing the word, the "n" word, you know. I didn't really know what it meant, but it sounded bad. I think I knew it was bad.

Later, in the car on the way home, my brothers were asleep, I was in the middle, in the backseat. I liked it there because I could talk to my parents. I was the kind of kid who always asked dumb questions, so I asked my parents about it, about my uncle using the "n" word, and they got really upset! My dad said I should never ever use that word and that my uncle was ignorant and backward. He was my mom's brother, so then she got really mad, because he was insulting her brother, and she started saying that where my uncle and cousins lived there were a lot of problems with Black people, and you can't blame him for being angry. My parents got in this big argument about it! My mom was like, maybe her brother never had a chance to make anything of himself and my dad said he had just like, taken the easy way out. And I felt so bad, just sitting there in the backseat wishing I had never brought it up!

But my mom, she is not a racist, and later she told me that she agreed with my dad, the "n" word was wrong and ignorant, and that it was sad that my uncle had never had more opportunities to be educated, but it wasn't his fault, but I should never use that word because only trash used it. And I totally agree. I have some friends who will say it's okay to use it if you're referring to people in general, not just Blacks. And they use it themselves, you know? You see Black people saying it all the time. I think if you use it to describe anyone who is lazy or criminal or on welfare or something, it's not bad.

I wouldn't use it though, because it's too harsh, even if you're using it to apply to trash. The whole slavery thing, you know? And the South, how bad it used to be. I think it's wrong not to learn from the past and try to improve. There are a lot of white rich kids here who just sponge off their parents and don't have jobs, and it's like, how is that any different from welfare people? I think if you call them the "n" word, it wouldn't be racist. It's racist to use it to stereotype one race, you know? But only rednecks and ignorant white trash people do that. And there aren't really a lot of kids like that here. Well, some, but I just ignore them if I can.

Laura was one of the first students I noticed at Laurel Canyons. She caught my attention early, in the second week of Advanced Writing, an elective that Elizabeth taught for seniors who planned on pursuing a college degree. I was struggling to learn student names and was taking pages of field notes, trying to capture my experiences and first impressions. On the day I noticed Laura, she was sitting next to me, expressing obvious disgust toward one of her classmates, Sam, who had refused to stand for the daily flag salute. Sam announced to the students sitting near him that he didn't believe in saluting the flag. He wasn't into patriotism.

"If he wants to be so pessimistic, he should try living in Africa where they have no freedom," Laura muttered when she heard this. She had long blondish-brown hair, curled at the bottom, and serious blue eyes set deep in a round, childlike face. She glanced at Sam with an air of superiority, then opened her folder and took out a neat, double-spaced laser-printed essay in preparation for the first draft workshop of the term. The assignment asked students to describe a significant event, memory, or moment in their lives that forced them to see the world differently or in a new way. Laura glanced at me and smiled. I smiled back: "What did you write about?" I asked. She handed me her essay, titled "Life Isn't Fair."

"It's about last year, when I didn't make the varsity softball team, even though the coach himself was like, I qualified. But my dad was all, the coach played to school politics and like, he ended up favoring all the kids whose parents gave a lot of money to the Boosters. It was totally unfair, and it taught me that hard work doesn't always pay off, because I worked so hard at tryouts and I still didn't make it, which wasn't fair. So like, I talk about how my dad always taught me that hard work and a good attitude was everything, and I believed that, and I still do, but sometimes, because people are unfair, you don't always get ahead."

In the desks next to Laura, two students, Tiffany and Emily, flipped noisily through a book of college scholarships. "All the scholarships are for minorities! I can't find one for white Presbyterians like me!"

"See, that's what I mean!" Laura said to me, gesturing at the scholarship catalog. "Like that! People are always trying to get something for nothing, and it's not fair. I don't believe in handouts."

"See if there's any money for being a redhead," Emily said. She had dark auburn hair.

"They aren't interested in that kind of minority I don't think, but let me see . . . "red-headed Presbyterian from Crimson"; that describes you, right? Except you don't go to church." Tiffany pretended to scrutinize the list of scholarships. "No, I don't see any."

"Maybe you'll have to get a job then!" Laura said, with an earnestness that seemed to miss the tone of the conversation. She turned back to me. "My essay is about that, like how, some people take the easy way out. There are too many people looking for handouts already, you know?"

When I got home that night, I checked the background sheets I had collected from students on the first day of class: Laura lived in Crimson, an affluent community just a mile from the school. She was a straight-A student and identified herself as "white" and "middle class, with enough money for things but not snobby." Asked to describe her experiences with multiculturalism, she wrote, "In my opinion it's very important to not judge people based on skin color. But I think they go too far sometimes."

This beginning—my memory of Laura, sketched here briefly—is an important origination—a creation and a kind of ordering. It provides not only the familiar ethnographic trope of the researcher's arrival in a new setting (Abu-Lughod 1993, xv) but also a particular construction of Laura herself: in Laura's background sheet, in her familiar insistence on hard work, in her remark about Africa, an easily recognizable profile of a problematic whiteness emerges. In this construction, Laura's beliefs—the racist undertones of her comments about Africa, scholarships ("handouts"), and people who "go too far" in their emphasis on racial equity—emerge from her position of racial and economic privilege. This familiar ordering—racist beliefs that stem from socioeconomic positioning—frames many of the tacit and explicit explanations of racism in the scholarship on whiteness. Here racism is posited as the result of either socioeconomic status (Laura, in this view, is protecting her privilege in the socioeconomic order by dismissing calls for racial justice, which she senses would threaten that privilege) or socioeconomic disenfranchisement, a psychosocial "wage" that compensates for a lack of class status and perhaps provides Laura with feelings of superiority that are otherwise hard to come by in the social, economic, and academic hierarchies of her school and community.

But Laura's story about her first memory of learning about race provides an alternative and less familiar ordering than the one I offered above. It suggests, for example, that troubling racism sometimes exists alongside staunch objection to racism. It suggests that *anti*racism, like racism itself, can be just as powerfully used to gain class privilege, to locate someone in hierarchical socioeconomic terrain. It suggests that antiracism can serve as a marker of class distinction. In this sense, the subject of Laura's parents' argument in her story is not about racial others at all but about the status of Laura's uncle, the "wrong side of the family," and about how best to teach their daughter so that she remains in the right class. The powerful lesson Laura takes from this is that antiracism is a way of distinguishing oneself from the working class, whom she refers to simply as "trash" in her narrative. As we will see, she often takes a strong stance against racism in class discussions and in her writing to ensure that she is not associated with this group of whites. But most important, Laura's story locates the roots, or beginnings, of her beliefs about race in emotioned structures of family and feeling as much as in calculations about economic or racial advantage. Laura's narrative, like many of the stories about racial learning that students told and that I share in this chapter, is a disorderly text, and as such it makes it difficult to pin race on class in the expected ways, to explain racism by way of class privilege or disenfranchisement. Britzman (2006), writing about the genre of the *bildungsroman*, notes that texts about one's own learning are "novels of affected psychology and affected education; they may be read as narratives on the passions of learning and not learning but also as points of entry into understanding the work of trying to know the self and the Other" (x). Laura's story, seen in this light, is a place of entry into the emotioned work of a racialized rhetorical world where labels like "the 'n' word" are steeped in deeply local, even familial, meanings.

In providing an up-close look at the goings-on of the English classes I observed at Laurel Canyons, I foreground ethnographic constructions of race and, especially, understandings of the origins of racism: the ethnographic, pedagogical, and racial orders, or texts, we construct. At the same time, I highlight Laurel Canyons students' emotioned constructions of race and of the origins of their own racial learning. In this chapter, via a discussion of methods and an introduction of focal students and ethnographic contexts, I attempt to challenge these orderings by focusing instead on what Britzman calls individuals' "remarkable, runaway, affected subjectivity" (viii). In doing so I offer a critique of various kinds of typification—ethnographic but also racial—and the theories that emerge from them. As Abu-Lughod writes, such typification is central to ethnographic projects and to our understandings of race, but it risks making "others" seem simultaneously more coherent, self-contained, and different from ourselves than they might be (7). "Generalization," Abu-Lughod writes, "however useful for other projects, helps make concepts like 'culture' and 'cultures' seem sensible. This in turn allows for the fixing of boundaries between self and other" (7). The students I introduce here and their contradictory stories subvert concepts like "whiteness," "privilege," and "racist," making it difficult to construct the usual categories of good (progressive) whites, on the one hand, and bad or racist whites on the other. It is this subversion of terms that necessitates the rest of this book, as I search for alternative ways of understanding the racism these students and their peers sometimes espoused.

To disrupt the processes of typification that undergird representations of whiteness, I employ a methodology designed to focus more carefully on individuals than on "culture" and one that uses narrative and the techniques of literary writing, a choice that is connected to my commitment to understanding beliefs about race as both emotionally and institutionally meaningful. Whereas ethnographers generally seek to reveal cultural meaning-making processes, I wanted to explore individual meaning-making processes in the context of schooling. Rather than aim for understanding the meaning of whiteness or race at Laurel Canyons, I focused on the meanings of racist discourses for individuals. "Narrative renderings of social life" (Hicks 2002) at Laurel Canyons seem best suited to capturing "complex particularity—the histories, attachments, practices, and meanings" (Hicks, 12) that are involved in individual discursive choices and investments. Following Holland, Lachicotte, Skinner, and Cain's (1998) description of "ethnographies of personhood," I aim to understand the "linked development of people, cultural forms, and social positions in particular historical worlds" (33).

Like Abu-Lughod, whose work on narrative ethnography I draw from here, I wanted the material generated by my time at Laurel Canyons to be able to speak to a set of debates about racism and critical education, but I also wanted to "let it be more" (xviii). Thus woven throughout this book are interviews with students, including their "beginning narratives"—

memories recounted during interviews that focused on comparing students' previous learnings about race with the ideas they currently encountered in their class—and their responses to texts that introduced or raised questions about matters of social difference, particularly race. Beginning narratives illuminate the interface between "intimate discourses, inner speaking, and bodily practices formed in the past and the discourses and practices to which people are exposed" in the present (Holland, Lachicotte, Skinner, and Cain 1998, 32). As part of the methodology of an "ethnography of personhood" they allow a window into the relationship between an individual's position within racial and class-based hierarchies and institutions and that individual's private, idiosyncratic, emotion-based processes of meaning-making. At the same time, beginning narratives raise questions about how we create order—temporal and causal, narrative and pedagogical—in our understandings of racism.

The vignettes and stories that I share in this chapter get at several ethnographic necessities: they set the ethnographic context of Laurel Canyons; they provide a narrative of the first few weeks of school, thus setting up my story's beginning; they create what Van Maanen (1988, quoted in Lindquist 2002, 20) calls an "impressionist tale"—a narrative account designed not only to orient the reader to the particularities of place and people but also to affirm the truth that narrative is in some ways best suited to render complex social terrain. Following Lindquist, I use an impressionist's tale as a narrative text "woven from actual events" but created to be a synthetic story, deliberately constructed to convey "both the complex and the predictable."

In the sense that the narratives here are taken from actual events, conversations, and dialogue that I recorded as an ethnographer, they are not so different from the transcripts in later chapters. Transcripts are, of course, representations, created accounts of actual events. But the purposes of the two types of representation are different. The narratives inevitably suggest emotional tone and mood; they set a scene and attempt explicitly to evoke particular responses in the reader. Transcripts are less able to do this kind of rhetorical work. Because this ethnography focuses on emotion, narratives help convey emotional complexity; they take us into the problem, as Britzman writes, of the emotional experience of learning and not learning and into the question of how the emotions are used (x). In the transcripts, in contrast, my intent is not to convey emotional complexity but to analyze it.

Of course, ethnographies are themselves narratives, and so I crafted, reconfigured, and juxtaposed stories, scenes, interviews, and student writing to make this narrative speak to my particular concerns. Following Abu-Lughod and other ethnographers who work in or on the borders of ethnographic fiction, I adopted many of the techniques of literary writing.

I did not construct events or people but tried to make scenes, dialogue, and stories flow smoothly, and I played with temporal relationships, moved scenes, interviews, and dialogue to disrupt the sense of order—temporal, causal, racial—readers might expect. Drawn to J. Stewart's (1989) argument that ethnographic fiction is ideal for understanding "the inner lives of people" (8) and for getting at subjective areas of inquiry such as race and racism, and convinced, on a more practical level, that altering details of time, place, and person was the only way to ensure participants' confidentiality, I edited, altered, moved, interpreted, juxtaposed, and selected to portray the complexity of the factual truth. I played with narrative to explore and exploit its possibilities. I also altered details that potentially revealed participants' identities, seeking to make participants anonymous even to readers familiar with the community, such as the students' teacher. In this sense, my ethnography is also a transparently created story, one deliberately constructed to convey the complexity of students' literacy experiences with, rhetorical constructions of, and persuasive investment in ideas about race at Laurel Canyons.

Of no less importance are the editing and constructing I did to manage the practical issues of readability. Dialogue in quotation marks was taken directly from field notes and from audio recordings. I cut uninteresting, repetitive, or unnecessarily complicating sections of conversations, scenes, student writing, and interviews. I deleted, from quoted dialogue, repetitions and the tics of speech that make literal transcripts difficult to read. I occasionally changed or added words, such as when students relied on context to supply meaning (when, for example, they used names that referenced people, practices, or places the reader is unfamiliar with). In the transcripts in later chapters, such editing was kept to a minimum.

The forms of data collection and analysis I used reflect traditional methods of qualitative inquiry. I drew on multiple sources of documentation to record, construct, and analyze my observations at Laurel Canyons. I wrote field notes, ultimately filling three spiral notebooks. I participated, in a limited way, in classroom activities, as a support for students and for Elizabeth. I often brainstormed with Elizabeth as she constructed assignments and activities, and we talked often about individual students and their learning. I interviewed students on multiple occasions, both formally and informally. I kept copies of student writing and classroom assignments, as well as of curricular guides and other institutional materials. Classroom field notes were reworked into narrative form as part of the first step in writing about my experiences at Laurel Canyons. These narratives, as well as many of the original documents, were analyzed and reanalyzed throughout the writing process, as I constructed my interpretations of them.

In the first part of this chapter, I narrate several days in Advanced Writing, a course in Laurel Canyon's open-tracking system that was billed as a class for students who expected to go to college, although only about a third of the students enrolled in the course had plans to attend four-year institutions. In this class students read, discussed, and wrote about several texts, including Maya Angelou's *I Know Why the Caged Bird Sings* and John Edgar Wideman's "Our Time" from his book *Brothers and Keepers*. This part of the chapter introduces two students, Ashley and Laura, and their responses to Angelou's book. Rarely explicitly racist, Laura used antiracist discourses as a way to shore up her identity as middle-class and to distinguish herself from "white trash." Her careful condemnations of racism often seemed aimed at denigrating her working-class peers. Ashley, on the other hand, consistently expressed racist points of view, attributing many of her ideas about race to her older brother, who, she said, spent time on neo-Nazi Web sites and was virulently racist. But Ashley also expressed disgust at the racism and classism she encountered in school (often neatly collapsing the two and focusing on race as the more available category), and at times antiracism emerged as a mode of resistance to what she perceived as elitism in the school. As a working-class student, Ashley was also a victim of racism, as other students used racist discourses to police the borders of middle-class whiteness that students like Ashley sometimes inadvertently transgressed.

The second part of this chapter describes the activities taking place in Introduction to Humanities, an English course required of all students at Laurel Canyons and the place where students completed their "senior projects," a passing score on which was necessary for graduation. This section focuses on two students, Mike and Michelle, and their experiences in the class. As students in Humanities completed the first assignment, their "life philosophy" posters, Mike, Michelle, and their classmates deftly circumnavigated a curriculum designed, on the one hand, to encourage students to reflect on their own identity and life goals and, on the other, to prod them to complete the Byzantine requirements of the senior project, a high-stakes graduation requirement involving a research paper, community project, and oral presentation. In class and in interviews, Mike could be counted on to voice a crude racism that other students shied away from or only confided in whispers. But he also often employed a highly resistant, critical discourse that called into question the "politically correct" pieties and middle-class values of the school, which included antiracism. He employed racist discourses in consciously resistant ways to parody and mock the middle-class mores forwarded in school. But unlike Ashley, Mike lived in an expensive home in a wealthy neighborhood and both his parents had college degrees.

Michelle, the final focal student, was also sometimes explicitly racist in class discussions and in interviews. But her racism, like that of Mike and Ashley, often blurred into a critique of school practices that she believed marginalized her because she was, in her words, one of the many unnoticed "average" students at Laurel Canyons, students who stayed out of trouble but didn't plan on attending college. As she put it, "I'm not a hick, and I'm not going to college, and that means there's nothing for me at this school. You have to either be wearing a cowboy hat or like going out with one of those hicks, or be studying for your SAT [a college admissions test]. Why should I care about any of this [the curriculum in Introduction to Humanities]? It's not going to help me get where I'm going."

As I highlight the prevalent and problematic ways students talked about race, a mosaic narrative underscores my efforts to unravel class-based explanations of racism, to disrupt categorization of Mike, Laura, Michelle, and Ashley as unidimensional figures at one end of the socioeconomic spectrum or the other, either as working-class dupes in need of pedagogical intervention and enlightenment or as privileged promoters of the racial status quo who are serving their own self-interest at the top of the social hierarchy. The students' stories about the beginnings of their awareness of race bedevil such labels of cultural analysis, complicating our sense of the socioeconomic benefits we believe race confers on those at the supposed top of the hierarchy and the psychological wages it is believed to offer whites at the other end of the socioeconomic spectrum. At the same time, the narratives suggest the ways in which racism was rooted in emotions that were in turn supported by school itself, a point I explore more fully in chapter 3, and by the rhetorical framing of antiracist pedagogies, a point I explore in chapter 4. These narratives begin in multiple places, and as such they unravel abstractions about racism and complicate the categories we construct in our analyses of it.

Demographic Contradictions

In the curriculum at Laurel Canyons, students could choose from advanced-placement (AP) history and art history, residential electricity, and consumer math. Peer groups in the school bore class-saturated student-devised names: The "rednecks" wore western-style shirts and cowboy boots and often, though not always, lived in the rural townships on the edges of the district. The "main group" (some students referred to this group as "snobs"; others said they were "popular" or "snooty"; some noted that this was the only real clique in the school, the only group that wasn't open to everyone) came from affluent homes, were known to wear expensive designer clothes, and were the leaders in many school activities. The "normals" constituted the largest group. These were students who appeared to be a toned-down version of the "snobs." They participated in school, got good grades, followed the social trends in terms of dress, and generally tried not to stand out. All four of the focal students considered themselves to be part of the "normal" group in school, though their peers' assessment was different: many students told me they considered Mike to be "popular"—perhaps by virtue of his participation in football and other high-profile sports. Ashley and Michelle were considered "kinda but not really white trash," in one student's words. They didn't consciously embrace the western style of many of the rural and working-class students, but they weren't part of the "normals" either. Most students considered Laura to be a normal, but a few noted that she was a "wannabe" popular kid.

Although Laurel Canyons was a suburban, all-white school, many students occupied complex social class positions: Mike lived in a big house in one of the wealthier subdivisions but hadn't seen his mother for six years. In his words, she was "white trash." He worked two jobs, at a drive-through window and at a clothing store in the mall. Ashley lived in a mobile home and had no plans to attend college, but she took all high-tracked courses and got straight A's in school. Michelle lived in a rented condominium in an affluent gated community with her mother, a single parent who worked as a paralegal. Laura, like Mike, came from a relatively affluent family; she lived in a large home in a gated community, and both her parents had college degrees. But despite high grades and AP credits, she planned to go to a local state school for college and live at home, to save money. The high school building itself suggested suburban prosperity: at the time of this research, it was only a few years old, with state-of-the art athletic facilities, a theatre, an art studio, and a large library with computers and a number of periodicals. The classrooms were well appointed with books, computers, and artwork. The teachers were credentialed, experienced, and committed to their students, serving as advisors for a variety of extracurricular activities and attending the school's theatre, musical, and athletic events. The school's Web site boasted that 77 percent of its graduating seniors sought postsecondary education.

And yet, as I'll explore in more detail in chapter 5, for most students, "postsecondary" meant community college, local business administration programs, beauty school, or technical classes that led to jobs in computers or mechanics. Local four-year state campuses, as well as the public state research university just twenty miles away, were the most ambitious postsecondary destinations; only a handful of students attended these schools every year. Of the few students who planned to attend four-year universities, none ventured out of the state, except to attend Christian colleges in nearby states or a state school in a neighboring state, still only a few hours' drive from home. Virtually none of the students aimed for Ivy League or well-known competitive admissions schools such as Berkeley, the University of Michigan, and New York University.

In the following sections, I try to flesh out these contradictions as I render my relationship with each focal student, blending interviews, descriptions of Laurel Canyons and its activities and practices, students' backgrounds and perspectives, and classroom scenes.

Laura's Story: Everyone Should Focus on the Positive

I followed Laura to her writing group, where we were joined by three other girls: Brittany, with large dark eyes, and the lively Julie and Heather, who were quick to jump into small-group conversation and always eager to gossip and giggle. It was early September; school had just begun. The students were still dressed for summer: tank tops, jeans, sandals, hair in ponytails. The morning was bright outside the wall of windows in the back of the classroom, and the room hummed with new-school-year energy. The students had written drafts of the first essay assignment: to describe an event or person that was significant to them in some way, that made them see the world or themselves a little bit differently. A full page of directions and exhortations, written in Elizabeth's preferred graceful font, had been handed to the students in the first week of school. After some preliminary chitchat, the girls decided to discuss Brittany's essay first. It was titled "I Saw Everything I Ever Wanted to Have," and it described a romantic struggle with a boy from Carville, a neighboring township of working-class whites near Crimson, where Brittany, Laura, Julie, and Heather lived. The boy was from the wrong side of the tracks, and Brittany found his charm hard to resist. Laura knew about Carville. "It's not a good place, trust me," she said to me as the girls settled down to read. "You wouldn't want to drive through there at night."

With a surprising flair for drama, Brittany described in her essay meeting, falling in love with, and then being duped by a boy from Carville who "used" Brittany for her money: "He told me that all along he knew who I was before he met me. He said he had no idea how rich I really was, but when he saw my house he saw everything he ever wanted. He said he saw his dreams, not me, he never loved me, only my money and reputation." In the draft, Brittany puzzled over this turn of events: "I had never once considered myself rich. Compared to his house and where he lives, I would say we are a little more upscale and less city-like (ghetto), but not rich." She concluded with the lesson she learned from this experience:

> What I learned from this was the power of money and social class. My mom never liked Tyler because of where he is from, or what social class he is in. Tyler wanted so badly to be in a higher social class that he hurt me like that. I consider my mom a pretty fair person (except when she grounds me!) but she immediately judged Tyler thinking he was bad because his family was not very wealthy. She was right to think he was bad news because he ended up being bad news, but from the start, she didn't like him. Tyler's friends didn't like me because they said I wasn't like them, but they never gave me the chance. I think money is a great thing to have a lot of, but money can not buy happiness, and too much will prevent it. I strongly believe that we are all people no matter how much money or anything else we have, and we all want the same things. I thought everyone was equal, and I thought that everyone else thought everyone was equal too. That is the other thing this experience taught me. Not everyone believes the world to be a fair place where everyone is equal. I am now a lot more careful about who I trust, and I never, ever invite anyone over to my house.

"So," Brittany began after the girls finished reading. "Did you get my point? Did it come across?"

"It's totally easy to follow. Like, we're all from the suburbs here. We get it."

"I was trying to be all, like it doesn't matter where you're from. Carville is a ghetto. You can't walk through there. But even there people are concerned with money, just like in the suburbs, and like in Crimson."

"It's like we think it doesn't matter because we're all from suburbia—white, rich, yuppieville." Laura rolled her eyes.

Julie added, "The suburbs are so boring! We're all the same and we think everyone is like us."

"But," Brittany countered, "white suburbia has changed. I saw this documentary movie about skinheads in suburbia. It was scary."

Julie, whose essay documented a trip to the Caribbean last summer on a charity mission with her church's youth group, added, "When I went to Jamaica, you're the minority. It was freaking me out. You see a white person and you're like 'Thank God!'"

"Now you know how they feel. Why they stick together," Brittany added.

"I think the point of this essay is don't meet people from Carville! In Jamaica they had big black bugs. I would just cry every time I saw one. Get them away from me!"

"I think a lot of people who live in Carville just don't try," Brittany suggested. "They've given up, and they just feel like, whatever happens, happens."

"My parents work really hard," Laura agreed. "They can afford a nice house for our family because they worked for it. I don't think it's bad just because only white people live there. It's not like all skinheads or something."

Tony and Jacob, in a neighboring group, overheard. Jacob turned to join the discussion: "You don't see it, but, like, it's there, racism."

But Tony said, in a definitive tone, "Yeah, but, you've got to understand, like, Blacks are equal and have the same opportunities. There is no difference between the races. Everybody can make it if they try."

"It's not like it's that easy in the suburbs, anyway," Laura agreed. "People work really hard, and it doesn't mean you're rich."

Jacob shook his head. "It's there, like a built-in advantage white people have."

"Maybe there's racism, okay, fine," Julie said, "but it's not like . . ."

"You see it at this school!" Heather interrupted. "Kids will say stuff."

"But that doesn't give Black people the right to complain," Laura insisted.

Jacob and Tony turned back to their group, and Laura began flipping through Brittany's draft. She pointed out some grammatical mistakes—a typo in the second paragraph, a confusing sentence on page 2. "Just make sure it's organized, and use spell check," she advised.

"Does Mrs. Reed want a title page?" Julie asked. "Because you might want to make a separate title page. You know, with everything centered."

Laura turned to me, "Do you know if she wants a title page?" Although I had briefly explained my research project and collected permission slips, throughout the year students seemed to see me as some sort of teacher or aide. I shrugged. "I doubt if it's that important, but I'm not sure."

Laura and Heather retrieved the assignment sheet from their backpacks and began to read portions of it out loud. "It doesn't say anything about a title page," Heather reported.

"I'd make one anyway," Laura advised, "just to be safe."

"Everyone's exactly alike in Crimson," Laura told me later that fall. "It's like white people everywhere, and a lot of Christians. It's a really great place to live. I always feel really safe." Indeed, Crimson was 99.3 percent white, with a slightly higher median income than the district generally (most families made more than fifty thousand dollars a year), and a slightly higher rate of college completion (32 percent). Almost three quarters of its residents were born and raised in the state, many of them descendents of original

German and Irish settlers. Although Laurel Canyons served affluent townships like Crimson, the district as a whole was not as wealthy as neighboring suburban districts. The school's proportion of students who qualified as low-income—living in households below the federal poverty level—was 5 percent, well under the state average of 26.8 percent but higher than the percentage for other suburban districts in the area, where the poverty level was as low as 3 percent. Most of the students lived in homes their families owned. The number of adults in the district with at least a bachelor's degree was 26 percent, above the state average of 17 percent but still surprisingly low. Roughly 75 percent of the adults in students' lives had not gone to college or had attended only sporadically, without accruing enough credits to graduate. Laura wasn't bothered by the racial and class homogeneity of her town. "It's not like anyone's stopping you from moving here. If you can afford it, you can move in."

Laura understood her family to be middle class because of her dad's job—he worked in the city for a company—and because of their house in Crimson. But she believed that she and her brothers weren't spoiled rich kids like some of her peers at Laurel Canyons. She and her brothers knew how to work, Laura said often. She had had an after-school job for over a year and had been babysitting to earn money for school clothes since she was twelve. She planned to live, when she grew up, close to home, in a house in her neighborhood or one nearby. She didn't think she'd ever move far away and didn't want to live in a city. "Too much crime," she said. She figured she would work as a teacher or maybe a paralegal, and she wanted to get married and raise children of her own.

She worked two school nights a week, plus one or two weekend afternoons. The money paid for her car and school clothes. "Kids who don't work are going to have a hard time with time and money management when they get to college," she told me as we talked about her job at a fast-food restaurant. Working did make her tired though, and sometimes she wasn't able to finish all her homework when she got home from work. "A lot of times, though," she added, "you can economize with studying. The teachers cover almost everything in class, so you don't even have to do the reading most of the time." She attributed this to the school's liberal open-tracking policy, where any student can choose to take any class, which meant, in Laura's words, "that the bright and the not-so-bright are mixed in together, which is a big problem with education today. Without tracking, it dumbs everything down. The teachers have to, like, accommodate the slow kids and slow down their lessons and repeating the same point over and over again. Besides, it's, like, no secret who's who around here, who the bright kids are, who the losers are. Not having tracking doesn't hide it. A lot of them advertise it on purpose with redneck clothes, and they sit there in class and glare at the brighter kids for making comments and having answers and being more intelligent, and then they walk out of class and scoff at us for being dorks."

She had one friend, Gina, who was an exception to this generalization. Gina tried hard in school, but she "looked like a redneck most of the time," Laura told me. "And she lives in this, like, tiny house with four kids and her aunt living there, and it's like there is no privacy at all. We can't even hang out."

"What makes Gina different from the rednecks?" I asked.

"She has good role models," was the quick reply. "Her parents, like, work all the time, just as hard as like my parents do, and if you see examples of your parents working hard, then you're going to work hard too."

When discussions of race came up in class, Laura was adamant that racial identity mattered "only if you let it. . . . Like there's one girl [in this school], she's Black, and she's really popular, and extremely stuck-up. You try to be nice to her and like, no one's good enough."

"Do you think there's racism?"

"No. People try really hard to have equal opportunity for everybody. Like with Angelou and Wideman? They made it. It shows anyone can, if they try."

Like several of her classmates, Laura often complained about Advanced Writing. In her view, it wasted time, making things more complex than they really were. She and two other girls in the class sometimes clashed with Elizabeth, who downplayed grades (deferring assigning them until mid and final portfolios), emphasized constant revision, and refused to provide students with easy formulas for writing. Laura also didn't like many of the assigned readings—The Catcher in the Rye, I Know Why the Caged Bird Sings, Lewis Nordan's Music of the Swamp, Wideman's "Our Time" and other essays from Ways of Reading, and a batch of poems Elizabeth had selected. Laura felt that the readings were about "people who complained all the time." When the students read Catcher in the Rye, she was frustrated by Holden's lack of responsibility: "I hated that book! He just whined all the time, and was really irresponsible, and his language was vulgar. I don't understand why Salinger would do that, make him talk like that. It's offensive. . . . I like to read. But when you read a book, you want to feel good for the rest of the day, okay? I like simple things. I don't like making everything so complicated all the time. Sometimes a story is just a story. There is no deeper meaning. If there is, I don't care about it."

On a warm Monday in late September, the students discussed their responses to Angelou's I Know Why the Caged Bird Sings.

"This is a story about a messed-up kid, like all the stories we read in this class. We should keep this bird covered!" Sara said to the students sitting near her.

"At least," Ryan responded, "Maya is an optimist. That last guy [in *Catcher in the Rye*] complained way too much."

"Totally!" Laura agreed. "Maya didn't criticize everyone. She was trying to be positive and make something of herself. It gave you a feeling of hope at the end. She got raped, but she didn't just give up and say bad things about the guy who did it to her."

"Actually, she seems to blame herself for most things. She thought it was her fault. That's another thing I like about the book. Holden Caulfield? He was always saying it was somebody's else's fault. He never wanted to take responsibility," Sara said. The students were forming small groups while Elizabeth handed out a list of discussion questions. "Who is Angelou's audience in this book?" Laura read aloud from the sheet.

"She was kind of like a teacher," a student observed tentatively.

"I don't know. I sort of wondered, did you think she was racist?"

"Totally. Like I kept noticing, she capitalizes *Black* all the time but not *white*. That's totally racist. It's not treating everyone the same."

Tori turned from another group. "I do think she's kind of racist. She bad-mouthed white people like at the revival. She's all like Black people will overcome someday. Maybe she needs to learn to be more tolerant of white people."

"I think she started off as a racist, but she learned to be tolerant. She focuses on the good things and tries to be tolerant of the people who wronged her."

"She assumes we need to be tolerant. But like what are we supposed to do with that? It's all white people at this school. Who are we supposed to tolerate?" Hannah asked, from the neighboring group.

Rich agreed. "She made everything into some kind of social problem," he said, "instead of looking at the individual."

"She's totally stereotyping," Julie said. "Every white person is just white trash. That's not a fair picture of white people."

"It's reverse racism," Rich said again, without moving his head from his arm, stretched out across his desk.

"I think it's hard to tell though. We're not Black. How do we know if she's being racist? None of us are Black," Heather responded. She often stressed the importance of an open mind.

"Just because you're not Black doesn't mean you can't tell if something's racist."

"She capitalized *Black* all the way through. She never capitalized *white*. It made me mad."

"Dude if some white author capitalized *white* and not *Black*, everyone would be all, like, that's really racist."

"I agree," Sara said. "I think they believe that white people owe them everything. And the thing is, most white people, their ancestors didn't live here at that time. They got here way after that. So it wasn't anybody in my family's fault."

Elizabeth, as she often did, allowed the students to continue without interjecting her own perspective or trying to redirect them, a strategy that she acknowledged didn't always lead to an immediately antiracist, or even logical, result. But it was a strategy—letting the students own and direct both class discussion and their own writing—that she believed in and that was supported by the educational theorists she studied, especially Paulo Freire, whom she had read in graduate school. She often talked about her belief in a Freirean student-centered pedagogy of empowerment and change.

"You guys are missing the point," Laura said. "I think the book shows that she's learned to be tolerant of white people. Like yeah, maybe she hated us when she was younger, but she learned and got past it, learned to forgive. I really liked this book. I thought it was very positive and optimistic. I don't think she's racist. I think that's unfair. You know. She's just trying to tell her story, and I think it's wrong to judge her."

In her journal, Laura wrote,

> But resisting the urge to follow the stereotypical, "I was a victim" quest for pity that many authors do, Angelou presented herself in a way that did not beg for pity. Such as when she discusses the rape, she does not damn Mr. Freeman. Instead she resists the temptation to pass judgement on the people who wronged her. . . . For the most part of the book, I could fully relate to Maya. . . . She does such a great job of setting up the situation; she makes her audience forget the fact that she is a homely, black, girl from the Deep South. . . . Maya's genius is in making the story seem so simple. I admire Maya for her optimism. When white children treat her badly, she doesn't judge or hate them. This made me see her as an intelligent, sophisticated person.

On a gray day that winter, I interviewed Laura. It was wet outside, the rain ticking against the windows, the humid, muffled light from the fluorescent overheads casting shadows. We sat at one of the Formica tables in the school library during sixth period, Laura's study hall. Her blue eyes were serious, but at various points throughout the interview—when she was annoyed or angry—they flared with a determined intelligence. Occasionally, they sparked with a sharp-edged humor. Her canvas backpack bulged on the floor in between our chairs, and on the table between us she had laid out a notebook and pen, reflexive school habits.

"Some of your classmates thought Angelou blamed white people for her problems. What did you think about that?" I asked, knowing that Laura had defended Angelou.

"Yeah. I know. I think, though, she might have, in the beginning, blamed them, but she learned to be tolerant of whites. She learned not to judge them. And I really respect that about her. I think everyone at this school should read this book. It would show them that if they take responsibility and work hard, it will pay off. All the people who don't want to do that around here? They kids who don't care, the rednecks and druggies—you know who they are, just look around—a lot of them are just bringing down the level for everyone else."

One interpretation of Laura that emerges from the narrative I've provided suggests that Laura's insistent erasure of Angelou's race and her desire to distance herself from "others" of all types, including her working-class white classmates, is a strategy that allows Laura to avoid confronting truths about racial inequality that would call her own privilege into question. Her need to distance herself from working-class whites shores up her own identity as a middle-class person and protects the privileges incumbent to that identity. Even her refusal to criticize Angelou might be seen as part of this strategy: by praising rather than criticizing Angelou, Laura positions herself as a "good" (antiracist) white.

But this reading of Laura draws a causal line from Laura's race privilege to her response to Angelou, a line that ignores the mediating, interconnected vectors of schooling, institutional experiences, and emotion that also play a role in persuasive processes. As we'll see in chapters 3 and 4, Laura's response to race often arose from her attempts to enact emotioned rules learned in other school contexts. We can hear, for example, echoes of a common emotioned rule at Laurel Canyons in Laura's comments about kids who don't care. At Laurel Canyons, "caring," "taking pride," and "taking responsibility" were often-repeated values attached to feelings of superiority and were used to motivate students. "You wouldn't want to end up like that," Julie, the inclusion teacher, often said, in reference to any person or group who appeared to be failing in some way. Laura's stance toward "the rednecks" and "druggies" may be classist and may serve on some level as a way of policing the borders of middle-class whiteness, which ultimately protects Laura's white privilege. But it is also a stance derived from lessons learned in school, where the fates of students who don't perform or conform often figure in a pervasive, fear-based motivational rhetoric. Similarly, Laura's insistence that the strength of Angelou's memoir is that it erases Angelou's blackness enacts a highly valued emotioned rule about the importance of seeing commonalities rather than difference. Unpacking these rules and their influence on Laura's discourse makes it difficult to construct Laura as a promoter of racial hierarchy, who is trying to ensure her own privilege. It also makes problematic any interpretation of Laura's racism as arising from an ignorant lack of exposure to difference or hostility to racialized others. All of these factors are at work on some level, of course. But teaching Laura differently will require attention as well to the underlying emotioned dimensions of race and to the ways those dimensions are scaffolded by school.

Ashley's Story: They Want White People on Their Knees

On the third day of discussion about Angelou, Elizabeth began by saying, "We've talked a lot about whether you liked or didn't like this book, and how the narrator of Angelou's story compares to the narrator of *The Catcher in the Rye*, and people are doing a good job getting past those judgments, you know, where Holden Caulfield is just a crazy messed-up kid and Angelou is from a messed-up family. Today I want us to focus on the sense of the audience, who Angelou's audience is for this book, and I think that thinking about that will help us sort through the issue of race that is addressed in this book. Okay, so if you look at your discussion questions for today, they're about audience." Elizabeth raised her voice as the students anticipated her next instructions and began shifting desks and backpacks. "So let's get into your reading groups and share your journal responses, and then dive into these questions."

In a quiet group near the back of the room, Ashley propped her head on her hand. "Did you guys, like, do the journal entry on this one?"

Heather, Rich, and James nodded. "I love this book," Heather said. "It was like a novel where you can't put it down."

"No way. It was boring," Rich said. "It was totally boring. Hated it. I barely read it."

James held up the discussion questions. "Anybody have any ideas on these?" he asked.

Ashley read the first question out loud. "'Who is Angelou's audience for this book? Who does Angelou imagine she is writing to?'"

No one jumped in, so Ashley took a stab at an answer:

If you really think about it, who is she speaking to? She's speaking to white people. She's sort of like writing the book talking about how racist they were and trying to make white people feel guilty. Like I could get into a bunch of stuff about it. Like how, yeah, slavery was wrong, but we apologized for that. And now there's no more slavery that we still have knowledge of. And we're still hearing about it. I mean, I don't know. The stuff you hear about on TV, some people, not all of them, but some of them are just we owe them the world, and we can't continue to make up for slavery. This book is like that. It's like, oh, you should feel sorry for us. And it's never going to be okay. But now they can go to school, and they aren't denied opportunities all the time. It's illegal now to deny them. So what more do they want? And this book is like, it's never going to be okay, and I don't agree. It's illegal. Black people want us to get down on our knees. That's what I think. And I think Angelou was trying to say white people are never going to be good enough, and we're better than you because of the past.

The students nodded in agreement. Ashley continued: "The message I get from this book is it's white people's fault. It's like, oh, I'm going to whine about this and talk about everything that happened to me. It's race. She wants white people on their knees. It's like she's saying, 'look at me, cracker, you don't know my strength.'" This last line Ashley picked up from reading a draft of another student's paper before class began.

Tori nodded. "She like, gets her strength, to put the blame on other people, for like, her problems and stuff. But she doesn't realize how, like that is not really going to work in the long run. It just weakens you, if you like, blame people for your problems. You have to rely on yourself, and be all like, it's up to you, if you want to succeed.

Sara added, "I agree with Ashley. I think they believe that white people owe them everything. And the thing is, most white people, their ancestors didn't live here at that time."

"If anything," Ashley continued, "we know what it's like to be her, because during the Holocaust, Poland was taken over by Hitler, and we're Polish."

"She feels like, the whole racial issue, I think she's trying to ask too much, she's asking for you to feel sorry for her. . . . What was that one part, she said that she . . . she was raped?" James asked.

"She was raped," Ashley answered. "And then she sat there and lied about it. She went to testify in court, and she didn't tell the truth. She lied, and says no. And then she walked away and was all upset."

"Why did that bother you?" I asked.

"Because I would have told the truth. White people get raped. You know? She doesn't stand up for herself."

"But she wants others to stand up for her," James said.

"The message I get from this book," Ashley repeated, "is it's white people's fault."

Ashley lived in a mobile home in one of the rural communities on the edge of the district, bought her school clothes at Wal-Mart, and planned on attending a sixteen-month business administration program upon graduation at the end of the year. Her skin was marked by splashes of red—a persistent rash that was the result of chronic poor health: two liver transplants before she was five and a series of problems with the medication her transplants required. Despite her vocational aspirations and working-class background, Ashley self-selected into all the college preparatory classes at Laurel Canyons and did well in them. She told me repeatedly that her family is "upper-middle class" and her home is not "trashy like you might think." Her parents did not have college educations. Her father managed a brake and muffler shop, and her mother did not work. Her sixteen-year-old brother, she said, was "really prejudiced" and spent all his time on the Internet at sites like "whitearayanresistance.com," but her parents, Ashley maintained, were not racist at all and hoped that her brother's ideas were just a phase that he will eventually grow out of. Her mother was deeply Christian, though in Ashley's words, "not a nazi about it." Still, Ashley reminded me often that her family didn't believe in evolution, and she was adamant that homosexuality was a sin that would be punished by God: "We're religious people and believe in living a good lifestyle."

Families like Ashley's constituted the northern, more rural part of the district, and many of them felt increasingly defensive about the subdivisions and "yuppies" that moved in during the past several years. There was talk of seceding from the district and a sense that they were being pushed out. This perspective cropped up in Ashley's sometimes trenchant analyses of the socioeconomic prejudices she saw in the school's peer culture. She spoke easily of the popular students who lived in big homes in Crimson, of students who shopped at expensive stores. She rejected her father's suggestion that her mother get a job as a cafeteria worker in the high school because "I wouldn't want my mom to have to deal with the kids here. They can be cruel and rude."

Again in the library, on that gray winter day, I interviewed Ashley. I asked her about her favorite readings from Advanced Writing. "So," I began, "what did you think of the readings in Mrs. Reed's class? Which did you love? Which did you hate?"

"I loved Walker's writing," Ashley offered, referring to "In Search of My Mother's Garden," which the students had just read. "She talked about how Blacks were discriminated against, but she didn't seem to me to be blaming anyone because she didn't mention names and didn't specifically say that white people were the ones at fault. I think she used a lot of voice to describe what it was like for Black women in the past. I felt really bad that it had to happen, but I think that it ultimately makes the women stronger in their battles against prejudice."

"You felt bad about what?" I asked.

"Like racism, discrimination against certain people, everything we've read about in this class. It's, like, I wish there weren't organizations like the Ku Klux Klan, because they make everything worse. You know my date [for an upcoming school-sponsored dance] is half-Black. Did I tell you that already? He's from Lincoln, which is not a great school, over by Westinghouse? You know where that is? But he's so nice and I met him because one of my brother's friends knows his brother. And he's going to the dance with me, and it's going to be great, but of course my brother has to say nasty things like "Oh, you're going with a mongrel.""

Later, Ashley wrote a journal entry on racism:

[T]his bothers me because I hate prejudiced and racist people. I wish we didn't ever have slavery or hatred in our country but unfortunately there is nothing we can do about it because it is here to stay. . . . I recently had a talk with my neighbors about it and they told me all these stories about when they were young in the south and what it was like for black people. The only thing different about them is the color of their skin. What is the big deal? I don't agree with the teaching of Ebonics in schools because we all should really be able to speak English here in the United States but what is there to do when black people are still regarded as not as important as white people? In my church it is taught that God created us all equal and his law says we are to be brotherly and kind but apparently God is no longer our Master. I think that we need God back in the world in order to stop prejudice and hatred. . . . One of my good friends was teasing me because I am going to the school dance with someone who isn't purely white. I told her to mind her own business. . . . I'm not like anti-white or anything because I am white myself but I don't agree with racism. . . . The only way we can really end our racism problems is for God to come and take us away.

When I asked Ashley to describe what she first remembered about race, she talked about the social stratification that she sees in school:

My first memory? I don't know. I can tell you one memory I have that will always stick in my mind, when I was going into like in seventh grade or something, about thirteen, whatever grade that is. And my family, we're middle class like everyone at my school. We have a house with three bedrooms, a living room, dining room, kitchen. It's a mobile home. Some people might call that a trailer. But we are not trashy at all. We're not poor. My dad is the manager of a car service shop, and my mom might get a job in the cafeteria at one of the schools, but I don't want her to, because kids are ignorant, really ignorant, and I wouldn't really want my mom to have to deal with that. Anyway, we're not poor, but one day I was in the yard of our house, and these girls walked by, and I don't want to talk bad about them, but they were kind of snooty. They go here now, you can see them in the hallways because they are so tan, they spend all their time and money—like how much would that cost—at tanning beds and wear skimpy clothes to show off their skin color. Which, if you think about it, is funny because the story I was going to tell you about these girls is that they called me the n-word! They said "you live like a _____!" And it's funny to me now, because, look, they're the ones who are obsessed with skin color and like getting really dark. And it's April, and I'm still as white as ever.

Ashley's story, like Laura's, is saturated with raced and classed significations. Reading it in the context of her other comments about race poses interpretive challenges. We might note, for example, that her more problematic comments—that Blacks want white people on their knees—emerge in all-peer contexts, while the disavowals of racism in her journal are aimed at a teacher audience. We might also note the ties between Ashley's precarious class identity—working-class but trying to fit in socially with more privileged peers—and her comment that Blacks want whites on their knees. In creating this us-them dichotomy in her discourse, is Ashley trying to position herself more solidly as "one of us" against "them"? Seen in this light, Ashley's stance toward race seems predicated on class—a defensive response intended to ward off threats to Ashley's tenuous grasp on her white privilege.

But an understanding of the emotioned rules taught at Laurel Canyons complicates this interpretation of Ashley. For example, Ashley enacts emotioned rules about "feeling equal" in her critique of Angelou: she criticizes Angelou for appearing to assert that Blacks are better than whites. Students were often told by teachers not to "feel special" or better than everyone else ("What makes you so special?" one administrator said when recounting to me his advice to a troubled student). It is interesting that this rule contradicts the one in play in Laura's response to Angelou, which exhorts students to feel separate from and superior to those who don't try hard enough or don't succeed. One rule uses feelings of superiority, the other uses feelings of shame. Both corral students who threaten to resist or refuse to conform. And both are applied by students to matters of race with racist effect.

Thus, as with Laura, it is tempting to read Ashley's comments as stemming from racism rooted in class identity and struggle. But without attention to how her comments also derive from emotioned rules, and without an understanding of how school practices both teach and enforce these rules, we will be unable to persuade Ashley to view race differently. Indeed, Ashley's memory of racial learning suggests that Ashley has grasped that white skin color and race privilege don't always go hand in hand. Her skin may be white, but her story suggests that race privilege is not much of a weapon at Laurel Canyons, a point about which I'll have more to say in chapter 5.

Mike's Story: Everybody's Racist, If You Think about It

Elizabeth told me, when I began my research at Laurel Canyons, that I could expect the Advanced Writing students to be, for the most part, serious and thoughtful. They had self-selected into an elective, college-bound writing class. If I wanted a real taste of the students at Laurel Canyons, Elizabeth said, I needed to observe a course required of all of the students. Such a course, she said, would have a much more carnival-like atmosphere. Indeed the contrast between Advanced Writing during first period and Introduction to Humanities during third was stark. I often joked to Elizabeth that Humanities was a zoo: the students were unpredictable, easily confused, irreverent, and boisterous, and the mandated curriculum—a hodgepodge of classic works of art and literature, popular culture, and the dreaded senior-project research paper—seemed designed to bring these qualities to the fore.

Early in the fall, in Introduction to Humanities, Elizabeth showed slides of famous artists' self-portraits—Picasso, Warhol, Chagall. In keeping with the first of the three themes of the course, "identity," students were to create their own self-portrait, as part of a larger assignment called the "life philosophy project." The project entailed a self-portrait, a written statement of beliefs about goals and values, and a presentation about a song the students were to choose to represent themselves or their lives. They were encouraged to use a variety of media—drawing, collage, writing—in their self portrait and to write their statement in their own voice.

"Ms. Reed, what's this for? These pictures?" asked Warren, as Elizabeth adjusted the slide projector. It was Friday, and the football players' lockers in the hallway were decorated with ribbons and signs: "Good Luck #72!" "Warriors Rule!" James, Mike, Nate, and Chris were wearing their football jerseys. On the desk in front of me someone left a flyer for a church: "Come share in our fellowship, this Friday at 4 P.M. The gathering will help you connect with Jesus Christ, the ONE who can make sense of this thing we call . . . life."

"It's for your growth and education, Warren" Elizabeth replied, in a tone that suggested wariness.

"Oh, good," said Warren, picking up on her tone. "I thought we had to write about them or something."

Other students were already at work, writing down a description of the portraits in their journals, as they'd been instructed.

Elizabeth put a CD in the player—the soundtrack from the most recent Romeo and Juliet movie—for background music while the students worked.

"You know this song has the F word in it, Ms. Reed?" Mike asked.

Elizabeth gasped in mock horror. "Oh, no! Call the principal! There's a bad word in a song! What are we going to do?!"

"Well, it's just, you know, I'd get detention if I was playing it," Mike said.

"That's a good point. What do you think about that?"

"I can't say, or I'd get detention for using a bad word."

Elizabeth laughed.

Warren pasted a picture of Bill Clinton on his journal. "Do you like him?" I asked.

He snorted. "No. Are you kidding?"

"Ms. Reed, should the journal entries be in order?" James asked.

"No, they don't have to be."

"Because if I don't get to one and then I go back . . ."

"That's okay. You can do them in whatever order you want."

"Do you want like your name and the date and all that on the top of each page?" Chris asked.

"No. It's your journal. Remember, you made them in class the other day? However you want to do it is okay."

"Are we supposed to just describe the picture? And that's all?" queried Michelle, as if she didn't trust the simplicity of the task.

"Maybe look at the background, too," Julie, the inclusion teacher, suggested. "That's what I'd do."

"But that will take like two lines."

"Maybe."

"So does this one picture have to have like 150 words?" One hundred fifty words is the minimum word requirement for each journal entry.

"Believe me, I'd happily stop counting words," Elizabeth whispered to me. "But do you think they'd write anything if I did? It'd be fifteen blank journals."

"No. It can be 150 words for both portraits."

"So is this entry 9 and 10 together?" Nate asked.

"Or should we put like 'Picture #2' as like a heading so you'll know we did both?" Warren again.

"You can do that, if you want to," Elizabeth replied.

"It adds to the number of words, so that's good," Mike pointed out.

Warren held up his journal, which was full of writing. "Look at that! I must be brilliant," he announced to the students seated near him. "Pretty soon I'm going to be teaching this class!" Michelle, Mandy, and James ignored him.

The clock ticked toward the bell. "Who has questions?" Elizabeth asked. "We have some time to discuss."

"When's it due?" Emily wanted to know.

"Does it count for senior project, or is that like totally separate? I'm confused!" Michelle yelled, above the departing din. Students were packing up, heading for the door, in anticipation of the bell.

"We can talk more about the portraits tomorrow," Elizabeth called, as the bell rang. Later that week, I said I admired her optimism. It's hard to teach here. "Yes, it is," she said, with her usual good humor. "Yes, it is."

A few days later, the students worked on their life philosophy projects by examining a series of quotations.

"Read the quotes on the posters, and write down your thoughts in response. Do you agree, disagree, and why? What does the quote make you think about? You can draw a response or write one, and you can also respond to things other people have written if you want to. Okay? Everybody ready? Do you have a pen or a marker? Warren? Did you hear the instructions?"

"Sure, Ms. Reed. You said it was okay to draw on the posters. You said it was okay!"

The posters were large white squares of butcher paper, with quotations printed on the top. They hung around the room like ghosts, curling upward at the bottom from the humidity. The quotations were supposed to introduce students to the themes of the class, spelled out in the official curriculum guide:

> [S]tudents will be given the opportunity to critically examine three main themes of our common existence, identity, justice, and mortality, by focusing on selected major texts of the 20th century (which may include drama, novels, short stories, poetry, non-fiction, philosophy, and film) and extended through a core of significant related music and art (which may include photography, painting, drawing, sculpture) of this same time period. Students will be required to read, write, and think critically about all aspects of the Humanities in relation to the common themes. Additionally, students will complete all phases of their Senior Project.

But first, Elizabeth told me during her planning period that morning, "I have to get them to think about what the humanities even means." She continued: "We could probably spend the whole semester on just today's activity, you know, trying to figure out what the quotes on the posters really mean to them." But she didn't have that luxury in this class, which in addition to covering the humanities, had to contend with the senior project. "We've got to stay on task in here, or the senior project will never happen," she said, shaking her head. "I don't know how we're going to do it all. It should be very interesting!"

The quotations on the posters included the following:

Literature challenges conventional wisdom and values. It asks us to confront those whom we usually do not like to meet.
Passive lives are not our own.
Only the educated are free.
The mass of men lead lives of quiet desperation.
All too often our choices are not our own. We never stop to ask ourselves what we really stand for, what we are willing to defend.
Nothing worth knowing can be taught.
The unexamined life is not worth living.

"Well-put," wrote one student, after the "quiet desperation" quote, in a bubbling purple script. "Sounds good," scrawled another. Several wrote simply "I agree" on every poster, even though throughout the activity Elizabeth exhorted students to explain their answers, to give details and reasons.

Some students argued with the quotes. On the poster that says "Only the educated are free," several students commented that in fact, education is quite expensive and there is nothing free about it. "Even public education is paid for by taxes," wrote the purple pen. Others took up the question of freedom: "Everyone is free, just not on the same level," wrote Mike. James agreed: "Everyone is free, just some people have more freedom of choice." Michelle pointed out that in addition to a lack of freedom, if you're not educated, you don't have as many options in life. "Good luck getting educated at this school," Chris opined.

Amy signed her name to all of her responses, and they all referred to her religious beliefs. About art challenging conventional wisdom, she wrote, in a tiny, neat script, "God's wisdom should never be challenged." On the poster that said "Passive lives are not our own" she wrote, "All life belongs to God." One classmate agreed: "Some people like being passive, because they know God is in charge." On the subject of an examined life, Amy wrote, "Life without Jesus would not be worth living." About making your own choices, she wrote, "Realize that God put you on this earth for a reason, and you will get far in life."

Michelle challenged the pessimistic tone of many of the quotes: "Life is always worth living!" The purple pen also took an upbeat view: "An unexamined life isn't always bad!" Michelle didn't buy Thoreau's description of the mass of men either. "Not true!" she wrote. "Those people just aren't trying to make something of themselves. Maybe some are desperate, but there isn't anything to prove this." Nate joked, "I'm quite loud, actually. I lead a life of loudness and manliness."

After the students finished writing, Elizabeth asked them to walk around the room and read what everyone had written. Then, she said, go stand next to the poster that you'd like to discuss further." Mike, Chris, James, Nate, Warren, and Tom headed toward the poster that said that "all too often our choices are not our own." They were joined by Mandy, Michelle, Sandra, and Jenna—almost all of the fourteen students in the class. "Look at that," Julie, the inclusion teacher, whispered to me, rolling her eyes.

"Okay," Elizabeth began. "Can someone tell us, first, what they think the quote means?"

Mandy said she thinks it means too many people influence what you're doing. "It's like people need to just be yourself. Don't be someone you're not, okay?"

Michelle snorted. "Yeah, like that's going to happen at this school!"

"Why did so many of you choose that poster?" Elizabeth asked.

"Because it was near the beanbag," Mike said. He was sprawled across it. Other students sat on the carpeted part of the floor next to him.

"No, really," Michelle said, "it's a big problem in this school. Thinking for yourself, you know? People just follow what their friends do. It's disgusting."

There were only a few minutes left, so Elizabeth asked the four students standing around the "Nothing worth knowing can be taught" poster to talk about their response to it and why they chose it.

"We disagree with it," said Amy. "Because why are we here?"

"You learn in school. That's what it's for. The teachers teach," said another student. The bell rang.

"Don't forget your journals are due tomorrow!" Elizabeth called as they headed out the door.

The next day, I asked Mike about the posters. "What did you think of that activity? Was it useful to you, or interesting?"

Chris overheard, and asked, "Are you going to use our opinions to help make the school better? Because it sucks!"

"That's kind of a tall order, don't you think?"

"I wish somebody would do something," he said, disgusted. "High school is the biggest waste of time."

Mike elaborated:

I thought the posters were pretty much just like everything else the good teachers try to get us to do, which is basically a waste, because kids around here, they don't want to have deep thoughts. Including me. I don't want to think about this shit. Why would I? You think we're going to Harvard or something? Most kids here, they're going to get the least amount of education, and the cheapest, which is like, pretty much the junior college . . . or like, my girlfriend, she's going to be a real estate agent, and you need a license and everything for that. And the only reason they're going is to get more money. Including me. If they could get jobs without going to college they would. So the teachers, like they should just give it up. We don't need this shit to make money, and everyone knows it.

The poster activity culminated a few weeks later with presentations by the students. They had made their own life philosophy posters, which included quotes, song lyrics, a self-portrait, and a "mission statement" expressing the students' beliefs about their purpose in life. The sample poster Elizabeth made about herself had a series of Andy Warhol–like metallic photographs of her face that emerged in differently shaded blue hues from a black background. The borders were edged with ribbon and quotations from her favorite authors, printed in a curving font around the poster. Attached to it was a short essay about her desire to work for social justice. Elizabeth hung her poster on the wall, along with all the students'. The thoughtful artistry she displayed in creating her poster sat in depressing contrast with many of the students': Nate drew a large hundred-dollar bill on his poster and put his picture in the middle of it. Amanda drenched her poster in pink, with a large picture of herself in the center in angels' wings and halo. Around the picture she pasted stickers of clouds, harps, and flowers. Josh put a Confederate flag on his. "It's not because of racism," he explained when I asked him what it meant to him. "It's because of my favorite band, Lynyrd Skynyrd." Tom put pictures of himself in various outdoor activities. In the largest one, he held a dead deer by the antlers, a rifle by his side.

Mike's poster avoided all of the clichés that plagued his classmates'. He did not pledge to work hard, live life to the fullest, be his own person, or focus on the positive. His poster was stark, with only one picture of himself in a football uniform. The picture was cut in half by a white path running through his face and part of his body. "My philosophy is about freedom," he began during his presentation. His voice was strong and clear. "I believe that it doesn't exist. There is no such thing as a free will. Everything happens in advance. For example, I don't come to this class because I decided to. I come because I signed up for it and it's a requirement. That all happened in the past, and it determines everything that happens now. You can't change anything, because you can't change the past. So I believe we should just relax and be happy, and realize that everything is already decided. You shouldn't worry because you can't do anything about it." He chose a song that I heard often on the radio that fall, by a hip-hop artist called Afroman. The song is titled "And Then I Got High." The lyrics describe how getting high interferes with the narrator's ability to accomplish the kinds of goals parents typically impose on teenagers—cleaning his room, studying for class, going to work. In the repetition of the refrain—"but then I got high"—a sense of futility emerges that was echoed in Mike's presentation.

Mike lived with his father and stepmother, a younger brother, and a sister who also attended Laurel Canyons. The family owned a large house in a new subdivision in Crimson. Like virtually every student I knew at Laurel Canyons, Mike worked part-time. (He had a job at a fast-food restaurant and a second at a clothing store in the mall.) He planned on attending a local state college in the fall. He was an athlete and had a high grade point average (GPA). He and his sister, like many of their classmates, were relentlessly calculating about school work, GPAs, SATs, and success. For Mike, all aspects of school life were funneled through this internal calculator: What will this get me? Does it make sense to expend x amount of energy, time, or money for the return I'm likely to get?

He liked to shock me with detailed accounts of the cheating that he claimed, and Elizabeth seconded, routinely went on at Laurel Canyons. "Smartnotes.com—you can't beat it. I haven't opened this book yet, but I've written every assignment. Smartnotes is really good. You can buy like essays and stuff, like really good essays; the outlines are free. You can buy stuff that's even better. Like if you want like a specific report, you don't have to write it at all. If you want something done for you completely, you can buy that. You can buy that for like ten bucks. And it's guaranteed, it's not even like the teacher knows because they write it for you."

Despite his seeming fixation on grades, Mike was not planning on attending a competitive-admissions college upon graduation. Both he and his sister wanted to stay close to home, and neither seemed aware of other possibilities outside the region or knowledgeable about what the competitive world of private school and Ivy League education can mean for one's earning potential later in life. Yet Mike's family was focused on the bottom line. His parents, he reported to me, supported his sister's forged excuse notes for the twenty-some English classes she had missed that semester, because she didn't need the course for graduation, so skipping it and getting a poor grade (she actually ended up with a "withdrawal" grade thanks to parental intervention and an administration that seemed to look away when parents asked it to) didn't affect her chances of graduating.

When the subject of race came up, Mike said he believed that racism was really just people speaking the truth, being brave enough to tell it like it is. "A lot of people are too scared to say what they think," he told me. "But it's bullshit, because we're supposed to be able to write our opinions, but then like nobody wants to hear it. All the bullshit about writing about your opinions and the whole, you know, 'be your own person,' in this school? It's basically bullshit." His racist pronouncements, as we'll see in upcoming chapters, were saturated with trenchant observations of the contradictions and hypocrisies of schooling. The "bullshit" he uncovered in "political correctness" was difficult to separate from what often sounded like a burgeoning voice of critical dissent.

Mike described his first learnings about race with his typical irreverence: "I was born knowing about racism," he began, joking. And then:

Okay, no. Seriously. You want me to be serious? Look around, at this place. I mean look around. Do you see any races here? I don't even know any Black people. How am I going to know about racism when I've never even met one? Well, hardly ever met one. I mean you could say I've learned about racism from my dad, but he's not really racist; he hates everybody. He's racist against the world: Black people, white people who are stupid and fat and lazy—and that's a lot of white people, let's face it—Indians—oh, excuse me, I mean Native Americans—and all people who don't speak English. He even hates French people because they're faggots, and he hates faggots too, and feminists, and lesbians, and Clinton. He really hated Clinton. I told you, he hates everybody. If you think about it, does that mean you're racist? Not really.

"What about your mom?" I asked.

My mom? My mom is a white-trash alcoholic. I was glad when she left. But my stepmom is real nice, and my sister—you know her? She's all pretty, and so-o popular. She and my stepmom, they aren't racist because they feel sorry for everybody. Most of the football team is racist, but who are they going to be racist against? It's all just talk. Basically, there are some rednecks and white-trash kids at this school who are racists, but everybody hates them because they aren't rich, except for like Chris, guys like him, he's a hick but still cool. And Chris isn't racist, either. So you can't really say. When it comes down to it, what matters to everybody in this school is how much money you have. Nobody gives a shit about the whole slavery thing, the whole politically correct thing.

I asked him again, when do you remember first learning about this stuff, about race?

"I told you," he said, giving me a grin. "I was born like this. Everyone in Crimson is born like this, if they were honest about it, which they're not. Only the rednecks are honest about it, and everyone hates them too."

Mike's memory of racial learning is brash, crude, offensively racist. He is casual and purposeful in his use of stereotypes and epithets. He was critical of antiracism and multiculturalism, which he dismissed as "politically correct." More than any of the other students, Mike's racism seemed connected to his privilege and his lack of exposure to difference and lack of empathy for others. As a white male with social capital in the school's peer culture, Mike embodied the resistant white student I often encountered in my own classes and often read about in the literature on critical pedagogy.

But as with the other students, Mike's discourses about race were enactments of values and emotioned rules in school. Indeed Mike dismissed discussions of racism because they were "pointless" and a waste of time. "This stuff is not going to get us anywhere," he often said. In this way, his views on race were no different from his views on many aspects of school. For all of his criticisms of Laurel Canyons, Mike thus echoed its values more overtly than any other student. As we'll see in chapter 3, instrumentalism—the idea that school was, or should be, preparation for the world of work and economic gain—was a prominent value in the school, with several embedded emotioned rules supporting it. In his criticism of antiracist educational efforts, Mike ultimately made a point in keeping with schoolwide values: there is no point in caring about things that don't hold the promise of bettering one's life. "If it won't help you find success, you should let it go and move on," one student told me. Mike applied this rule to the texts and ideas he encountered in Elizabeth's class and concluded that no one "gave a shit about that stuff" because no one cared about school beyond its connection to students' economic futures. What they were supposed to care about, Mike often reminded me, was "getting ahead in life. Nothing else really matters."

Michelle's Story: This Has Nothing to Do with Me

Michelle wore her blond hair pulled back in a tight ponytail, with thick bangs shading eyes that were usually carefully arranged in a hostile teenage glare. Her mother was single and worked as a paralegal. Her father, she told me, had a lot of money but usually didn't share it, although he was prone to occasional acts of rash generosity, like the red BMW that Michelle drove. "It's nicer than my mom's car, can you believe it. He is such an a-hole," she commented, as she described her parents to me. She lived in a rented condo with her mom and an older sister in one of the more affluent communities in the area. Her sister worked in a real-estate office. Throughout her senior year, Michelle did not make college plans. She hated school, she told me often. Neither her mother or sister had post–high school degrees, though her father had gone to college and wanted Michelle to go as well and her mother had taken courses in a local business administration college. She was not active in school-sponsored extracurricular activities, and she didn't take high-track classes unless they had a reputation for being easy.

Like Mike, Laura, and Ashley, Michelle was part of a seemingly undifferentiated middle in terms of her peer group at Laurel Canyons. But as she was quick to point out, "middle" hardly began to describe her. "This school tries to make everybody the same and it's like, give me a break. We're not all going to some fancy school or give a shit about philosophy and reading this shit. I don't know why we're here. It's the biggest waste of time." She waved one of Elizabeth's journal-writing assignments toward me. I glanced at it and read: "What does it mean to be successful? What does it mean to have a good life? What do you want your life to be like? Whom do you admire and for what?" It was supposed to help the students think about their identity posters and life philosophy presentations, due in the next week.

"What did you write?" I asked.

She flipped her journal toward me. The cover was decorated with a photograph of Michelle with the face cut out, leaving her familiar ponytail and black T-shirt. In the blue-lined notepaper showing through where her face would have been, she wrote in tiny letters, "This is me." I commented, "Interesting cover," having already learned that Michelle viewed direct questioning with suspicion. "She [Elizabeth] made us do it, so I was like, okay," she shrugged, refusing to comment more. I turned to the last page, where Michelle had written the required three hundred words on her definition of success and the good life.

> I think a good life is one where you are comfortable with what you have and you have enough to get what you want and not worry. You have your friends and family around you and they understand you for who you are, not for some fake person you are trying to be. I hate fake people and I would never want to be one. But it is hard because a lot of people don't really want to know the real you. Success for me would be having a lot of money and a nice car, and being true to my friends and family. It's most important in the end. The person I admire most is my mom. She goes to college at night and works all day so we can afford to live, because my dad (ASSHOLE!!) won't pay for shit (sorry Ms. Reed) and my mom, she has done it all on her own without taking a handout from anybody. Now I know I need 137 more words (Ms. Reed does this count?) so I will say something else about my mom. She is tough and is not afraid

to argue with people, which is another reason I admire her. She argues with her boss to get more money so we can have food on the table, and even though she sometimes rides a motorcycle (can you believe it!) she can still look very professional for work. She is not fake though. She is always true to herself and will tell you what she thinks even if you don't want to hear it. Sometimes I really hate my dad. But not my mom. So, in conclusion, success means being successful with money and also not being a big fake. I believe that is all I have to say. 301

Michelle's identity poster, like those of most of her classmates, revolved around a series of clichés, written in blue and pink felt-tipped pen, at angles across her poster. "My mission statement is about how we should be ourself," she began, when it was her turn to present her poster to the class.

Don't try to be someone you're not. Stand up for what you believe in. Don't be afraid to have chances, and relax and have fun. I picked a quote that says that there will never be justice if ordinary people remain silent, and I think that is so true. If you think about it, it's really true. If you speak up, you could have a hand in sending someone to jail, and helping our justice system. Criminals will go free if we just remain silent and let them get away with it. I think it's important to live one day at a time and to try to add something to the world. The song I picked is Mariah Carey's "hero," because you should be your own hero."

Warren fiddled with the CD player, and the song came on. He started to sing along.

"Warren, zip it," Elizabeth said.

Michelle threw herself back in her seat and gave a disgusted flip of her pony tail, clear signals of her general disregard for the assignment and the class. Elizabeth, noticing, reminded her, "Hey, you picked this song. I don't see what you're so mad about." Michelle rolled her eyes and ignored her.

The next presentation was Josh's. He wore his usual western shirt and cowboy boots. He was one of a handful of learning-disabled students in the class (four out of fourteen). "Most of these kids," Elizabeth explained to me at the beginning of the year, "do not have learning disabilities in the real sense of the word. Their parents have had them tested until some psychologist gives them the diagnosis. Then they get extra help in their classes, special homework assignments, and the big thing is, they aren't held to the same standard on the senior project, which helps them increase their chance to graduate. Josh is perfectly capable—the only thing his IEP [individualized education plan] says is he needs extra help with spelling and following directions. He's not ADD, he's not dyslexic. They just want to make sure he graduates." Josh ambled to the front of the room. He held up his life philosophy poster, with the Confederate flag displayed prominently in the center, a picture of Josh glued to the upper corner of the flag. He had printed the lyrics to Lynyrd Skynyrd songs around the edge of the poster. He mumbled quickly through his presentation, about the importance of minding one's business. This seemed odd until his chosen song came on, Lynyrd Skynyrd's "Don't Ask Me No Questions." As class was ending, I asked Michelle what she thought of his presentation. She flipped her journal at me again. "It's all here, if you want to read it," she said. Elizabeth required that students write an entry on each day's presentations. In her journal, Michelle had scrawled: "I was told we weren't allowed to use white pride in our lockers and cars. Didn't someone get suspended last year for a flag like that in there [sic] truck? So why is Josh using it in his presentation? Is it ok to use this flag? Because I thought it made people think you were racist. Even though it is ok for them to be all, Black history month, but we can't have white pride. That is called hypocrisy. How many words is this supposed to be Ms. Reed?"

In an interview later that year, I asked Michelle whether she liked Laurel Canyons. She shrugged. "It's okay, I guess. I don't know, not really. Lisa is really my only friend here. The groups are hard to get into. Even the rednecks, not that I would want to be in their stupid group, but it's like, what do you have to be to hang out with them? I guess dirt poor, which I'm not!" When I asked if she liked or had learned from the readings in Introduction to Humanities, she said they were all weird, and commented that it seemed "stupid" to read about race in a setting where there was no diversity.

"Do you think there's racism at this school?"

"Yeah, against white people mostly. No, seriously. I know that's like, politically incorrect or whatever, but, seriously, have you noticed, how everyone is all, the suppression of Black people, the suppression of Indians, and no one talks about white people?"

"Do you mean, like in Intro to Humanities?"

"Yeah. Exactly. What did we read in there? A book about poor Black people [*The Color Purple*]. A movie about a gay guy [*Philadelphia*]. A movie about Indians [*Smoke Signals*]."

"Well, you also read that play, about Picasso and Einstein and Elvis, and you watched *The Graduate*, and read *In Cold Blood*."

"Yeah. A book about murderers. And the play, and *The Graduate*, what does that have to do with white people? That's not about being white. It just happens to have white people. The others were about *being* Black, you know. And you can't talk about being white, or it's racist."

"I think that's a good point, actually. If you could talk about being white, what would you say?"

She snorted. "Like anyone would listen. I'd be all like, I'm not racist, and I've suffered too. My people have suffered. My mom suffers all the time, with work and going to school. And my sister. It's not like it's easy. And we're not rednecks either. We have enough money. And I'd say, you know, like it's not that easy, just fitting in, being average. It's like my mom says, the average kid gets overlooked, and I think that's really true at this school. I try to fit in, and where does that get me? This school is like, so trying to pretend that we are all these happy, like goody-two-shoe kids who can't wait to go to college, and they do all this crap trying to say, like, this is what you'll need in college. And it really just leaves you out, like me and Lisa. We're going to [a local community college], and my sister went there and she says you don't need any of the crap they pretend you do here. Maybe at [college] or something, I don't know. But what they're teaching, you don't need it."

A complex but clearly differentiated social hierarchy shaped Michelle's beginning story, much as it did Laura's, Ashley's, and Mike's. But Michelle's is interesting for the ways that it locates these issues in school. In the next chapter, I take up the relationship—between schooling and racism—that she raises, as I explore the "subterranean disciplining of emotions" (Boler 1999, 4) that took place in Laura's, Ashley's, Mike's, and Michelle's English classes and in the school more generally. Such "disciplining" has long been understood as a mechanism for teaching the values and habits of mind associated with socioeconomic class. But attitudes toward race were also learned via emotioned rules taught and enforced in school.

Here is Michelle's beginning story.

I had this friend in junior high. I didn't go here. We lived in Centerpoint, where my mom is from, then, and I went to junior high there, and we moved because it's kind of a rough school, you know? Not as good as here. But in seventh grade, me and this girl, Sheila, were best friends, and she was Black. It didn't mean anything to me. We had like all our classes together, and if it was alphabetical we sat by each other because her name was right after mine. I didn't have a lot of friends there, because there are so many losers who live in that district, which is why we moved. But Sheila was cool. And we hung out all the time. She was really funny and would always crack me up. And we got in trouble in class a lot, we would like goof around, mouth off to teachers, and they were always like calling my parents and stuff. And one day, we got in trouble . . . and the teacher sent us to different rooms so we would stop talking and goofing around, and to me she was like, why do you hang out with her? She's getting you in trouble. She was all, Michelle, you're college material, you're going somewhere, and she's not, and she's bringing you down. I can see it happening. And I was all, whatever. It still pisses me off. I guess she thought, like because my dad has money, and like went to State, that I was all "college material," but you know what? I'm totally not. And my parents, they're fine with it. My sister went, but I'm all, I don't want to leave my friends, and my grades suck, and I'm just totally not college material. And my dad's like, that's fine. I think he doesn't want me to leave my mom, because then he'd have to deal with her. And my mom thinks college is expensive for what it is, you know? You can get the same thing at [the local community college], or even better, they have really good teachers there, and it costs like half the price for tuition. My mom just wants me to learn something useful so I can get a job, and she's always all, Michelle, what are they teaching you at that school? It's ridiculous, half the stuff we read in here, it's not going to help in the workforce, and my mom knows it. I think college is kind of overrated, if you ask me.

The explanations we construct about the causes and origins of white racism tell only a partial story. These partial stories highlight the connections between race and class and suggest that racism is a result of privilege, an attempt to gain it or protect it. But these stories do not account for the institutionally scaffolded emotioned dimensions of persuasive processes, the contradictory, affective, idiosyncratic, and institutionally mediated paths by which students become persuaded by particular ideas about race. In the next chapter, I flesh out this analysis, looking at how emotions and schooling work together to give racist ideas their persuasive force.

3

EMOTIONED RULES TAUGHT IN SCHOOL AND
THE PERSUASIVE POWER OF RACISM
NOVEMBER AND DECEMBER

> There were times in Angelstown when I did fieldwork with people
> who seemed difficult and not very likeable. What was I to make
> of values and beliefs that seemed to run contrary to my own? It
> seemed to me that as long as I could summon a certain generos-
> ity, fieldwork could continue, but there were times when I came
> very close to stopping the pretense of generosity and walking
> away. I never took that walk, however, and now, at this writing
> moment, those same social scenes seem more illuminating than
> what I imagined back then. But I am left with this predicament:
> How does one textualize such encounters, such people? How do
> I render the density and subtlety of life lived if, as the observer, I
> felt that mostly nastiness and short-sightedness were to be found
> there? Call this my prejudice, but it seems to me that some of the
> most important human encounters are those that cause anxiety,
> even anger. At these moments, we encounter all those limitations
> that define us. Anxiety and anger may protect our most vulner-
> able places, but they also encourage us to root ourselves ever
> deeper inside limiting definitions that rationalize against that
> wilder stuff that calls to us from just beyond our narrow selves.
> —Ralph Cintron, *Angels' Town*

Throughout the autumn months at Laurel Canyons, I listened to the students talk about issues of race as they encountered them in texts. In between classes, during her planning period, Elizabeth and I sat in her quiet
classroom and discussed the students' progress. By late fall, we had glumly
concluded that from an antiracist point of view, we were far from success.
Indeed, the final drafts of the Advanced Writing students' essays on Maya
Angelou were not sympathetic to her claims about racism. At times they
were openly hostile toward her.

Reading through the essays during her planning period, Elizabeth said
November was always the worst month: the enthusiasm that marked the

beginning of the school year had waned, the weather was dark, and we were still months away from June. She had made copies of the essays for me, and we pulled two student desks together as we read, flipping through the pages and pointing out particular passages as we went.

"Look at Teresa's," Elizabeth said, without looking up. "On page 2, second paragraph."

I read: "[The book] talked about lesbianism without discussing the immorality of it, which is wrong. She almost seems to be racist herself, but towards whites. . . . She thinks that all whites are unreal. She said white people's feet were too small, their skin was see-through, and they walked on their heels, not on the balls of their feet. As we read this, we realize that she was just being silly and was not used to exposure around whites. Her point of view is very immature."

"Angelou is immature," Elizabeth said. "That's a good one." She underlined it. "I'll come back to this one. Any thoughts on how I should respond?"

I shook my head. "You're the teacher." She laughed. We were both already skimming the next essay:

> The first time I read it, I did not want to read that she was a lesbian. On second reading, I noticed the mention of prejudice between white and black. It was not a two-sided hatred though. Maya did not hate whites, she simply did not understand them. . . . The reason for the book, however, was not to tell a poor black girl's experience of being hated by the whites, but rather a story of a person just like any person, looking for acceptance. . . . The conclusion of the story was not about racism, though racism was mentioned quite a bit. It was about life going on. . . . Why does the caged bird sing? It is not (contrary to popular belief) to be annoying so it's captors will set it free. It sings because it knows life goes on.

I stopped reading and looked up at Elizabeth, ready to discuss.

"Just keep going," she said. "It gets better." I flipped to Ashley's, the next one in the stack:

> She puts herself on a higher level than the whites of this world and makes herself a victim, blaming everyone else for her problems. . . . Maya feels racial superiority to the entire world and doesn't care what happens to everyone else. . . . This novel is targeted toward everyone who is not black, didn't get raped, and is guilty of any injustice. In other words, it is a novel for anyone other than Maya Angelou and her superior black race. . . . These continuous realizations while reading reached a peak when all I wanted to do was be like "STUPID MAYA, YOU IDIOT, YOU LIAR, YOU SELF-CENTERED HYPOCRITE."

"I'm not saying that her writing this book was a bad thing, or that its full of lies, or that black people are full of lies, but this book seems very questionable," another student concluded.

Jacob wrote that he was sympathetic to the racism Angelou endured but took issue with her tone: "It was as if she was screaming *look at me cracker, I've experienced it all, no one knows my pain, no one knows my strength.*"

Laura avoided most of her classmates' critiques of Angelou and focused instead on Angelou's heroism. In her draft she repeated the points she made in her earlier journal entry almost verbatim: "Resisting the urge to follow the stereotypical, "I was a victim" quest for pity that many authors do, Angelou presented herself in a way that did not beg for pity. Such as when she discusses the rape, she does not damn Mr. Freeman to the hottest pits of hell. Instead she resists the temptation to pass judgement on the people who wronged her. . . . Maya does such a great job of setting up the situation; she makes her audience forget the fact that she is a homely, black girl from the Deep South. . . . I admire Maya though because of her optimism. When white children treat her badly, she doesn't judge or hate them. This made me see her as an intelligent, sophisticated person."

Reading the drafts, I pondered Cintron's question and the passage above: *How does one textualize such encounters, such people?* Cintron (1998) answers his question by translating what he sees as a human problem—nastiness, anger—into an ethnographic one. For him, ethnography begins with the assumption that emotions have a public dimension, that "anger and nastiness . . . do not just well up from the interior of a person but are distinctly shaped along systemic lines" (131). One of the points of this chapter is to locate the complexity of inner life within larger institutional forces. Like Cintron, I hope to deflect any interpretation that might otherwise pathologize research subjects as racist and instead to emphasize the workings of ideology: the emotioned rules taught via what researchers in education have long called the "hidden curriculum" of schooling—the taken-for-granted, tacit lessons learned, though not necessarily explicitly taught, in class. In the stories and analysis that follow, I have deliberately highlighted "nastiness"—the offensive, the problematic, the narrow, the stereotypical, and the prejudicial in students' responses to matters of race—in order to trace the origins of racism across time and contexts, moving between the interior and emotional, and the institutional and ideological in my analysis.

When Elizabeth and I finished reading, I commented on the racism that marked almost every essay. "What's your sense of how to address this?" I asked. "I mean, how as a teacher do you deal with this kind of racism?"

"It would all come crashing down in a heartbeat if I made too much of this stuff. We'd have parents, students, other teachers totally freaking out. It would be ugly! But the other thing is, I have to say, I didn't notice the racism, so much, without you here pointing it out. I'm not sure I would have really noticed it that much." She paused. "It's not that I don't think they're racist, don't get me wrong, or that it doesn't need to be addressed in these essays, but it's just, well, I guess what I mostly notice is that the tone and the critiques of Angelou are exactly the same as the critiques of Nordan and Salinger a few weeks ago—you know, just "he's crazy, why are we reading about this crazy person" or clichés and easy answers. No real confrontation with the text. So it seems hard to understand how it's really about race."

It has taken me a long time to understand fully Elizabeth's insight that day in November as we sat reading the students' responses to Angelou. In the rest of this chapter, I share that understanding by turning to a number of sources and sites. First, I propose a way of reading racist discourse that takes into account their affective, as well as political, texture. I use *racism*, *racist discourse*, and *racist language* interchangeably throughout this chapter to refer to language that relied on negative stereotypes of nonwhite groups, portrayed whites as more "normal" than or superior to other groups, denied claims of racism, denied that racism was a current social problem, or blamed the victim of racism for race-related problems. Such language not only insulates white people from confronting racism but also supports and helps to construct racialized social inequality. I then argue that racist language functions in a metaphoric way. An understanding of metaphor as a rhetorical device that links unlike things can help us understand how racist language connects common racist ideas and nonracist feelings, values, beliefs, associations, and desires. Racist discourses, this analysis suggests, are best understood as psychosocial rhetorical phenomena: forms of persuasion that must be understood not only for their political meanings and implications but also for their persuasive subjective coherence. As such, racist discourses structure feelings linked to but not reducible to the racial politics they forward.

To understand this phenomenon, I turn to an examination of what educational theorists have called "the hidden curriculum" of schooling to show how school scaffolds the rhetorical frameworks within which racist discourses become persuasive. I argue that part of what makes racist discourses cohere and thus what makes them persuasive is school itself—the tacit, taken-for-granted practices and discourses that exert a powerful but largely unacknowledged pedagogical force. The hidden curriculum teaches not only the habits and values of social class, as researchers have long argued, but also the rhetorical frameworks that make racism persuasive to students. I examine the way the hidden curriculum works at Laurel Canyons by way of "emotioned rules"—norms of behavior, ways of valuing and viewing the world that are taught via feeling. Emotion in this context must be understood as a discursive practice: "the words used to describe emotions are not simply names for . . . preexisting situations with coherent characteristics; rather these words are themselves 'actions or ideological practices' that serve specific purposes in the process of creating and negotiating reality" (Zembylas 2005, 937). More important, power is an integral part of all discourses about emotions because "power relations determine what can, cannot, or must not be true or false about them . . . Emotion discourses establish, assert, challenge, or reinforce power or status differences" (Abu-Lughod & Lutz 1990, 14, quoted in Zembylas 2005, 937). Because emotions are related to issues of power—indeed Boler (1999) and others have described schools as places that "discipline" emotions—I have examined emotion discourses at Laurel Canyons in terms of rules, and because these rules are part of the socialization processes of schooling, I have asked how these rules participate in the construction of persuasive discourses about race.

Like the rest of the book, this chapter is written in mixed genres: It begins with a series of scenes from the unfolding days of the school year at Laurel Canyons. These scenes not only illustrate and complicate the argument I make here but also lay bare the workings of that argument, its constructedness. In this sense the scenes speak to ongoing concerns throughout the book about how we represent racial subjects, how we address the question Cintron (1998) raises. They are tools with which to interrogate the assumption that our ethnographic, as well as pedagogic and educational, constructions name something that was already there. Toward this end, some of the scenes focus explicitly on student discussions of race and racism, but I've also included other scenes that relate to but don't directly address matters of race, to give the reader a sense of the day-to-day world of Elizabeth's classes.

In the second half of the chapter, I include more traditional ethnographic analysis as I examine transcripts of interviews and class discussions and use them to suggest an emotion-based theory of the persuasive appeal of racist discourses. In my analysis of the transcripts and the racism embedded in them, I asked,

What emotioned rules were taught and how were they taught?
How were emotioned rules enacted?
How were they applied and policed across situations and contexts?
How did emotioned learning participate in the development of persuasive beliefs about race?

These questions form the basis for the argument I make throughout: that what appears as racism in students' discourse cannot be used to infer racist attitude or belief on the part of the students. Instead, such discourses should be understood as emotioned rhetorical phenomena—forms of persuasion that gain their force through their elaboration in school practices that are not about race per se.

That fall, there was a burst pipe in the school—two hallways flooded and no running water in the main building. For three days, we slept in as repairs were made. We came back on a Friday, and then got Monday off for a professional development workshop for teachers. By Tuesday morning, the students were cheerful, surprisingly focused, and ready to work. In Advanced Writing, they tackled John Edgar Wideman's "Our Time," an excerpt from his autobiography, *Brothers and Keepers*. Elizabeth had photocopied the excerpt from *Ways of Reading* for the class, and the burst pipe gave students extra time to read it. Elizabeth was reinvigorated by the unexpected time off too and newly confident that with this text, students would start to "get it." "Angelou sets them up for this stuff," she commented before the class discussion on Wideman began. "It's not a great book. Wideman will be different."

"Our Time" weaves back and forth between Wideman's own story—he went to Oxford as a Rhodes scholar—and that of his brother Robby, who went to prison for robbery and murder. Elizabeth was determined that this text would move students past the easy answers they tended to rely on and would encourage them to examine their own identities, as well as the construction of identity in the text . The writing assignment for "Our Time" was divided into two parts. In the first section, students were asked to analyze "the dangers of explaining away the complexity" of Robby's life that Wideman grapples with in the text: "What does [Wideman] do in the writing of the piece that makes this story a complex one instead of a stereotypical one?" In the second part, students were invited to tell a story from their own life and to do so in a way that avoided "explaining away the complexity."

But on the first day of discussion, Laura commented that she liked "Our Time" for the same reasons she liked Angelou's autobiography. She enjoyed its positive message of hope and uplift and was glad it didn't get mired down in "complaints about race."

"I really liked it," Laura said, as students settled into class. "I thought it was good for a lot of reasons. It was a good story, and it had a good message about how the choices you make influence you and like where you end up. It was a lot like Maya, showing that like, the circumstances can be bad, but it doesn't have to hold you back."

"That's not really true though," Jacob said, turning in his desk. "I thought it was kind of about, you know, how race comes in, and racism kind of held back his brother, you know?"

"But it shows that race doesn't really matter. He doesn't even really mention race," Laura countered.

Jacob glanced at me. "He brings it up a lot, I thought. Like the whole thing about how his mom felt and how they dealt with racism."

"I read it as, his mom was really tolerant and didn't blame people. Like Angelou learned to be tolerant of whites."

Ryan agreed: "Race doesn't matter in this story. I liked how it wasn't all angry about racism and stuff, like Maya. That got really old."

Jacob flipped through the pages of "Our Time." "Page 533, if you read, like it says, 'Even though the strands of the net—racial discrimination, economic exploitation, white hate, and fear—had existed time out of mind, what people didn't notice or chose not to notice was that the net was being drawn tighter, that ruthless people outside the community had the power to choke the life out of Homewood.' And then, like a paragraph down from there, it says that his mom did hate people because of racism, and she was unforgiving."

"I don't know, I didn't really get that out of it," Laura said, in what seemed like a purposefully dismissive tone. Later, she would tell me that Jacob was an example of the "artsy" types at Laurel Canyon. "He thinks too much! It's like come on!" she said, describing him.

"What do you not get?" Sam said, from across the room. "The man is keeping them down, that's what it says."

"No, he's saying that they struggled but they made it. He's trying to understand what went wrong with Robby."

Before anyone could respond, Elizabeth called the class to order and directed students into small groups to discuss their first responses to the text. "If it's easier, you can start by discussing what you wrote in your journals last night."

"I'll start," Ashley said, fishing for the journal pages in her notebook. "I had like an okay response to this story, but I didn't love it." She read out loud,

Some parts of this were really good and some parts were very racist and annoying. I enjoyed the part where Wideman was describing his mother and how she would always give someone the benefit of the doubt. I thought that his mother has a very good outlook on life and it's a shame that the racism had to corrupt her thoughts. She was just a good person who got dealt a bad hand in life. When the racism problems happened and she changed her tune I felt bad because she seemed to give up her good morals so easily and that's a shame. . . . It seems as though Wideman was trying to excuse Robby, and it shouldn't be excused. It is a big deal to rob someone and take drugs. It's really bad because you can mess yourself up for life. . . . I felt bad for Wideman because he had a brother in jail and a bitter-hearted mother who now dislikes white people because of little things that happen to her and the other people in Homewood. . . . I thought this reading was not as rude to the reader as the last one [Angelou] but this one still addressed the opinion that white people are horrible and evil.

"If you write that in your essay, just to warn you, you'll get graded down," Laura said. "Seriously. You have to be all deep if you want a high grade from her. You can't just focus on having a positive outlook." She rolled her eyes. "It's like, I'm sorry that I'm not that complex. But that's the way I am. So how can you criticize that?"

"Exactly. I'm the kind of person that doesn't care. I just let things roll off my back. Like why get all worked up over something stupid? That's what we do in this class," Tori said.

"I totally agree!" Laura said. "We're all like, writing about society and pointing out all these problems and I don't see anything to criticize or delve into. It is what it is. I'm doing worse in here than I've ever done in any class. Everything we're writing about is so up in the air. I like things black and white, right or wrong."

"It is kind of sad," Jessica reflected, "like in what we're reading, to see the world like they do, like all full of racists and stuff. It's—I don't know—it is sometimes easier to focus on the positive."

"Why can't you be allowed to be optimistic? What is so wrong with that?" Laura demanded. "Like you're happy, and then it's like, if you look deeper, it's really nasty and sad and negative. So sue me, I don't get a good time out of like reading a book like that. I guess that makes me a bad person or something. I'm not deep, I'm just not."

"I don't know, I like reading and writing," Jessica said.

"I like reading," Laura agreed. "But not this stuff. I love romance novels! I read them all summer. But in here it's like, to have your opinion criticized and graded, it's just wrong. It takes the joy out of it. I don't want to look at myself, and my past and everything. My past was happy, I loved my childhood, end of story."

"Yeah, it's like in here we have to pick everything apart, and it's like, what if you don't want to?"

"I think the point of this class is to make people look deeper," Laura said. "But if people are happy just looking at the surface, then you should leave it alone. Because they're content."

"If you think about it, this class kind of discriminates against people who just want to be happy and focus on the positive," Ashley added. "Is that really fair?"

When I summarized this discussion for Elizabeth, who had sat in on a different small group that day, she shook her head: "They're impossible!" she said, with a mixture of frustration and humor. But we both agreed that as frustrating as things were in Advanced Writing, they were worse in third-period Humanities, where the agenda for that day was packed with multiple mandates from the official curriculum, including a lesson on thesis statements, some time for finding topics for senior projects, and a discussion of the upcoming justice project, which asked students to choose a current or historical case where, in the student's view, justice was not served. Elizabeth called the class together by asking students to write in their journals about possible topics for their senior projects.

"Ms. Reed how many words, how many words does it have to be?"

"I thought we had forty-five days for this part!"

"Can we just list the sources we have or do we have to write about all of them?"

"Folks, let's remember the purpose here. You're defining an area of research and a project that's interesting and valuable to you. That should guide your work. Your purpose." Then, as an afterthought, Elizabeth added quickly, "And your purpose cannot be 'so I can graduate.'"

"But that *is* my purpose!" Chris moaned, and put his head down.

"You should be finding out what your project is about. The time to be picky is on the works cited page."

Several students looked frustrated.

"Do we need to do a word count?" Michelle asked again.

"I need more library time," Nate said to Chris, under the chatter that continued.

"No, dude. You don't. There's a Web site called easybib.com. It'll find sources and cite them for you."

"We're so lazy," he said to me, as they got up and headed to the computers on the side of the room.

"Okay, people, I know you're confused about this. But remember, we will work this out in the next couple of days. When you're finished with your journals, pass them forward. We need to work on thesis statements for *Color Purple*. Your essays are due next week."

"What!! What is she talking about?" Michelle demanded in a panicked voice. "I don't understand. I thought we had till the twenty-fifth?"

"No, that's when the background investigation [for senior project] is due," Chris said from the computer. "Background investigation is for senior project, *Color Purple* is for . . . I don't know. It's just a regular part of the class, you know, like English class?"

"I hate this, I really do."

Elizabeth handed out a thesis worksheet. It explained that a "thesis statement, as defined by the teachers here at Laurel Canyons, is a clearly stated, researchable/supportable, debatable claim." She had included the part about "as defined by teachers as Laurel Canyons" for students' parents, who will use irregularities in the standards or curriculum as evidence in their complaints about a course their child is struggling with or a teacher who is failing their child. The caveat could be cited by administrators, who calmed such parents by telling them that the curriculum has been carefully designed by committees of experts and was applied fairly and uniformly in all required courses.

The students had to create thesis statements in their essays on literature and in their research papers for their senior projects. On page 2 of the guidelines was a list of steps for creating a thesis statement that refer to the senior project. Michelle pointed out the inconsistency immediately:

"I thought we were doing the *Color Purple*, and now we're back to senior project?? I don't understand this f—ing class."

"These are just examples, Michelle. They can apply to both writing about literature, which we're going to do shortly, and the senior project research paper, which we'll get to later."

On page 3 of the handout were sample statements that the students were to evaluate using the criteria on the handout. All of the samples were taken from previous students' attempts at creating a thesis for their senior project research paper.

"I believe that anyone who tries sewing will enjoy it."

"The idea that people should have more free time is very interesting."

"The FBI is a good career choice for people who want to fight crime."

"All people believe that O.J. is guilty."

"The quality of life in the U.S. changed dramatically with the discovery of electricity."

"This paper will explain how to repair a flat tire."

The second half of the handout consisted of thesis statements that met the criteria. The first example read: "The effects of drug addiction can have an equally devastating effect on the social, economic, and personal lives of the families of the addict."

"What is the claim being made here?" Elizabeth asked, trying to direct students to see the connection between the thesis and the criteria.

"Drugs are bad," James said.

"Well, yes, drugs are bad, but what's the specific claim being made in this thesis statement?"

"Drugs are addictive?" Michelle said, tentatively.

"In this thesis statement," Elizabeth said, and read it again.

"Drug use has a bad effect on your social, economic, and personal life," Ryan answered, reading partially from the handout.

"On who? According to this thesis statement?"

"On the family of the drug user," Mike finally said, sounding frustrated.

"Exactly," Elizabeth responded. "So we can see the argument being made that saves this thesis from just being a statement of the obvious, right? It would be too obvious to say that drugs are devastating for the addict."

"You could support that," Lisa pointed out.

"You need it to be debatable though. It's not just, is there evidence, but could you argue with it," Julie, the inclusion teacher, tried to explain.

"Well, for a lot of druggies around here, it is debatable," Michelle said under her breath, defending Lisa.

"Let's look at some of the problematic statements," Elizabeth said. She read from the list: "The senior project is an excellent opportunity to learn time-management skills."

"Now that's debatable," James said. Elizabeth laughed.

The next day, they began an activity using the death penalty as a case around which to create thesis statements. The activity was designed to reinforce the thesis work from the day before, but like most things in Humanities, it also had a secondary purpose, to prepare students for their justice projects.

"We're going to get in groups and talk about your initial opinions on the death penalty, whether you're for it or against it and why. What are your reasons for how you feel? Then we're going to have a whole-class discussion and put all the reasons on the board." There was a long, bored silence. The students slumped in their desks, looking bedraggled and disheartened. It was overcast again, and the darkness outside added to the air of dejection in the room.

"Come on, guys, it's going to be fun," Elizabeth added.

Hearing the note of resignation in Elizabeth's voice, Lisa perked up. "I agree, Ms. Reed," she offered brightly. "It does sound fun!"

"Thank you, Lisa. I appreciate your enthusiasm."

"You're welcome, Ms. Reed," Lisa giggled. Michelle rolled her eyes.

Elizabeth handed out a list of facts about the death penalty: dates, laws, numbers of executions by state, quotes from experts about crime deterrence.

In a corner near the beanbag at the back of the room, Tom, Mike, Chris, and I pulled our desks around to face each other. They glanced at the fact sheet. Chris put his head down.

"So are we for or against?" I asked.

"For," Chris said, not raising his head.

"I'm for it."

"Me too."

Elizabeth walked over to our group. "How are we doing?"

"We're all for it," I said. "Well, except for me. I'm against it, of course."

A flicker of interest crossed Mike's face. "How can you be against it?" he asked. He seemed sincerely perplexed. "If you take a life you have to be willing to give yours."

Tom also seemed surprised. "Wouldn't you want to kill the person who killed your family? They're given a chance to get a lawyer and all. They get a chance. Depending on how good your lawyer is. If we don't do anything about rape and murder, it's going to increase, you know? Once they know they can get away with it. Like back in the days, they used to execute people if they spoke against God, and you know what, a lot less people did, because they were afraid."

"I'm against freedom for people who don't deserve it," Chris added.

"But who gets to decide who deserves it?" Elizabeth asked.

"I just think you should be punished," Chris said, ignoring her question. "You gotta draw the line somewhere. Because we live in an imperfect world. In some like certain situations, you have to be against freedom. You have to draw a line."

Elizabeth moved on to another group. "You should be prepared to give your reasons" she said, over the slowly building sounds of life around the room.

"Everyone's entitled to his opinion," Tom shrugged, hearing Elizabeth. "There is no right or wrong."

"I think there's too many insanity cases," Chris mumbled, head still down. "Someone can get off too easy if they just say they're insane. Like Jeffrey Dahmer."

Elizabeth called the class back together. "Let's take a vote and then discuss reasons for both sides."

All of the students were pro–death penalty, except Michelle. "I'm against it because it's taking the easy way out," she explained. She waved the handout at the class. "It says here the death penalty is not a deterrent. That's because people know the death penalty is the easy way out. It doesn't scare them. Locking them away is better. I think if you're being sent to prison for life, then you shouldn't be killed, because that's too easy. You're not suffering if you're dead."

"I disagree," Tom said. "They don't suffer at all in jail. Look at the jail here. You have basketball courts and gyms. The cells are air-conditioned. They have so much free time, they sit around all day, do nothing. So we're paying for them to sit there and do nothing with their lives. Basically they get a free life." There was a ripple of agreement in the room.

"Has anyone actually been to a prison?" Elizabeth asked.

"It's true the death penalty is not very suffering," another student agreed. "Yeah, maybe you have the fear you're going to die, but once it's done it's over with and lethal injection is such a painless way to die, they swab your arm with alcohol before they give you the injection. I guess they don't want you to be sick when you go to hell."

"They used to jolt you, four thousand volts of electricity," Tom said, under his breath. Mike laughed.

"If they do it, you should do it to them. Whatever they did is how they should die."

"Why should we waste all the money, like taxpayer dollars, by having them sit in there for like twenty years or however long they live? Just kill them, it'd be cheaper."

The room had the vague feeling of a lynch mob. Elizabeth intervened. "Okay, people. Listen. Look at your handout. There were nineteen thousand homicides in one year and 293 people put to death. Who do you think those people were?"

"The ones they caught?" offered one student.

"No."

"The ones who killed the most people?"

"No."

"The unlucky ones?"

"Yes. Unlucky. Why? What separated them from the 18,700 or whatever who weren't put to death?"

"It's people who can pay. If you hire a lawyer, like O.J."

"Exactly. So is this fair? Does this meet your standards for justice?"

"But if someone killed your family, wouldn't you want him to die?"

"No," Elizabeth said. "I wouldn't. Here's the question to think about. Is this justice or is it revenge, and are those things the same thing? Or should they be?"

"What about someone who is a serial killer though? Don't you want to see them suffer?"

"Yeah, but dying is the easy way out," Michelle said, sticking to her point. "I think you should chop off his fingers one by one."

The day after the death penalty discussion, Elizabeth handed back journals.

"There's no way she reads all these," Mike said, thumbing through his, looking for the grade. "As long as you write something, you get the points." His journal entries contained reflections on the hockey season last year, interwoven with compliments aimed at Julie, the inclusion teacher, and Elizabeth: "I sincerely hope you two enjoy reading my journal," one entry politely concluded, after filling up the word requirement by writing down all the words to the Star-Spangled Banner. In another entry, he wrote about movie stars he wanted to have sex with, and then added, "I am just writing this stuff because I know you are not reading them all, the most you do is skim them. So I'm just going to say Ms. Reed is an intelligent teacher with great hair." *This gets you nowhere*, Julie, who read that batch, wrote tersely in the margin. Elizabeth and Julie did read the journals, but because some points were assigned merely for meeting the minimum word requirements, students couldn't fail on content alone. On content, Mike received twenty-four points out of a hundred. "Minimal thought, attention, investment, or commitment," Elizabeth wrote, justifying the grade. Some of Mike's most obnoxious entries, though, were ironic and thus did suggest a certain kind of thought and attention. Asked to write entries about his classmates' life philosophy presentations, Mike wrote,

> I would just like to start off by saying that I thought that all of the presentations were great. They all showed that they put a lot of time and effort in. First there was Dana. I thought she had a very positive attitude toward life. And I liked her song. You can't go wrong with Tom Petty. This was obviously a great choice, because Jason chose it too. They were both very original in their presentations. One thing I liked about Jason's project was that he decided that laziness would not stand in the way of his dreams. This is different than me because laziness is my dream. I hope to live each day accomplishing nothing.

About his own presentation, Mike noted that it was "definitely the most honest" in comparison with the clichés offered up by his classmates. Asked to write an entry about what was most important to him and how he defined success, he wrote, in a rare moment of apparent sincerity, "there are lots of things that are important to me. One of these is my country, and my friends. I think that to be successful you must have a few things. You need money, so you don't have to worry about paying the bills. I do hope that my life is more meaningful than this though. I hope my life is important."

Embedded in discussions like those just narrated were racist discourses— sometimes uttered casually or subtly, other times more overt. In the following sections, these discourses are examined as they are manifest in some of their most common forms—dismissal of critiques of racism as "complaining" or "whining"; the idea of reverse racism, individualism, and white racial superiority. I trace these discourses in two directions, linking them not only to institutional, pedagogical, and curricular practices that constitute a hidden curriculum of race but also to the private realm of individual but publicly and institutionally mediated emotion. My goals are to highlight how ethnographies of personhood can capture and help us understand the rhetorical construction of "nastiness," to use Cintron's phrase, as it is happening at the point of intersection between practices and people, and to help teachers and researchers understand how schools create frameworks within which "nastiness" becomes persuasive. Understanding, and ultimately changing, the emotioned rules that give rise to these frameworks is central to the work of persuading students to see race and racism differently.

In the analysis below, I first identify forms of racism—discourses that promote racism or insulate white people from confronting racism—in transcripts of interviews, small-group student discussions, and whole-class discussions and in student writing. I then trace those discourses through the emotional pedagogy of the school, asking how they were taught via the emotioned rules in place in school—commonplace exhortations, often repeated by students and especially teachers and other school officials, that attempted to manage student feelings. I also look at the manifestation of these rules in realms beyond spoken exhortations: in posters and other classroom decorations (happy faces on classroom furniture; buckets of candy handed round to "cheer" a slouching group of students; motivational sayings posted around the building, etc.). Finally, I analyze transcripts of student interviews during which I asked students to talk about what they saw as the meaning and value of a particular racist discourses, and I examine the connections between these interviews and the emotioned pedagogy of the school. The sections below thus attend to the connections among three kinds of ethnographic material: transcripts containing racist discourses, transcripts (largely from interviews) in which students explain their feelings about the discourses and explain what they meant to express through them, and observations of general school practices that taught emotioned dispositions. Each set of materials flows from the next. Although the sections range widely over ethnographic texts gathered in different moments in time, with different students and in different circumstances, each is anchored by the focal students introduced in the previous chapter—Michelle, Ashley, Laura, and Mike.

"They just want to complain": Denial or Rationalization of Racism

One of the most common student responses to matters of race at Laurel Canyons was an exhortation to focus on the positive, often coupled with an assertion that particular authors or characters complained too much about race. Students often remarked that they hated "whiners" and often refused to engage in discussions or analysis of texts by people whom they thought were whining: As Laura put it, "It's like, you hear people, all the time, and they're all, like racism has held me back and I'm suppressed, and I think, come on! Everybody's suffered, okay? White people have suffered too. But like, you don't run around complaining about it and whining all the time. That gets you no sympathy, in my book."

It is easy to see such claims in terms of the racism they promote. Criticizing authors of color for "complaining" or "whining" allowed students to dismiss claims of racism and effectively turned the tables, putting the writers, rather than the perpetrators of racism, on trial: "I don't like people for having bad attitudes," another student said. "Who wants to read about that?"

But examining the emotioned rules in play at Laurel Canyons helps unpack *why* these exhortations and the racism they supported were persuasive to students. Indeed, exhortations to focus on the positive were ubiquitous in the culture of Laurel Canyons. They framed complex and contradictory constellations of meanings and served unpredictable purposes for students, who based the value of positive thinking and avoiding complaint on an underlying sense of agency and feeling of hopefulness. Assertions such as "Angelou complains too much" and "Black people whine about racism all the time" were meant by students not necessarily to dilute or neutralize critiques of racism, though that was clearly a result of such claims, but rather to make possible a place for action and hope that students felt was necessary to their futures. This explanation appears paradoxical at first glance: statements such as "Angelou's a whiner" are clearly problematic from an antiracist point of view. But when I asked students to talk about such statements, they focused on the importance of a good attitude to their own future success and well-being, and they sometimes even extended this desire for a successful future to the author or character of color. In other words, for some students, pointing out that Angelou was whining felt like a helpful comment, a way to help her or other people of color move past racism, feel more hopeful, and find success.

The notion of "finding success" was linked to the strong instrumental focus of schooling at Laurel Canyons, a focus that was taught by promoting positive feelings, as well as feelings of control over and hope about the future. The following took place during an interview with Michelle:

JENNIFER: What if, actually, complaining was a good thing to do in certain cases, because it was a way to get something to change. Like if you don't complain about racism, how will we ever end racism? Right? Let's just say, like, complaining is actually a good thing. How would you feel about that?

MICHELLE: I don't think you can say, like, it would do any good, to just whine all the time. Like, around here, I know, it would get you nowhere.

No one would listen, and people would just be all, do the work and it will pay off. Like you can complain about homework, but the truth is, if you do it, by doing it, you are getting somewhere. You're getting a job or like college or whatever. And complaining, if we just complained and never did all the work, then like I think it's like just giving up and saying okay, I don't care what happens to me. And then, it's like, just hopeless, I guess. Just complain because nothing does any good.

The idea that complaining was a kind of giving up that led to feelings of hopelessness was taught almost daily in school via emotioned rules about the purpose of schooling that were used by teachers, administrators, and often students themselves to justify and rationalize academic practices that otherwise appeared pointless or useless and to give an energy and sense of purpose to activities that were routinely characterized by students as a waste of effort. Indeed, motivating students appeared to be a full-time job. "Cheer up!" Elizabeth often said at the beginning of a class period, as students slumped in their desks. She did her best to make the room cheery as well: there were bright yellow beanbags with smiley faces along the far wall of the classroom; she kept a bucket full of candy near her desk in the corner of the room. This effort to motivate was also reflected in the school: the hallways were often adorned with encouraging posters made by various student groups; and of course, there was the student aide who read the pledge of allegiance over the public-address system each morning, always ending her recitation with an upbeat "Have a great day!" Students were taught to avoid conflicts with each other and with teachers, and they were reminded that what appeared difficult or boring or frustrating now would pay off in the future. "I know you don't want to do it," Julie, the inclusion teacher, would say when a student complained or slacked off. "But think how happy you'll be when at the end of the day you've got that college degree and can make something of your life."

The principal, in an interview, echoed Julie's language as he talked about his efforts to make the curriculum less vocational and more focused on college preparation and to motivate students and parents, particularly those who came from rural and working-class backgrounds, to see education as a means for a better future. One of his goals for the school was to encourage more students to apply to college and to get students to aim higher in their postsecondary aspirations. Being overly passionate, angry, or confrontational was viewed as damaging to these efforts. As one administrator told me during an informal conversation that took place in the hallway in between classes, "Elizabeth's a great teacher; she's really passionate but almost too passionate sometimes." When I asked what he meant by "too passionate" he elaborated: "You know, it's great to have enthusiasm for this work, but when it spills over, or when people are getting really worked up, it can have a bad effect on motivation. It's hard to keep the kids focused, keep them focused on what we're doing, getting through the requirements, getting through the senior project, so they can get out there and really make something of themselves."

Students internalized these emotioned rules and put them to unintended uses, and as they did so, their language sometimes took on explicitly racist overtones. For example, for students, whites were seen as having an appropriately positive view of life, whereas people of color, in students' view, seemed not to understand the connection between a good attitude and a hopeful, successful future. The following interview with Ashley illustrates:

JENNIFER: Why does it bother you that [John Edgar] Wideman's mother is focused on racism and is angry about it?

ASHLEY: I just think it's sad, you know? She was a happy person, and she's letting this bring her down. And it will influence her kids. Like, what if Wideman just sat around complaining about race? He wouldn't have made something of himself and written a book and become successful, you know? A lot of people, like a lot of Black people, sometimes—and I'm not trying to be racist—but if you can't realize that you have to see the good, then they just get stuck complaining about racism and being all hopeless about things, and they let life pass them by.

These beliefs were structured into the emotioned universe of the school. Students were repeatedly told that their destiny was in their hands if only they maintained the right attitude. But such lessons, aimed at teaching students responsibility and even empowerment, had the unintended effect of cutting the legs out from under the critique that Elizabeth's pedagogy, and antiracism in general, requires.

White Victimhood, Reverse Racism, and the White Other

This section focuses on two discourses that promoted racism and that were scaffolded, unintentionally, by efforts in the school to create a multicultural curriculum and to promote tolerance. The discourses—reverse racism and white innocence—arose from curricular and pedagogical practices that were intended to teach against racism. The ideas of white victimhood and reverse racism included claims that whites were victims of racism and people of color weren't, that whites suffered as much oppression as people of color; that people of color were racist against whites; and that whites were unfairly blamed or "stereotyped" for racism when it was actually only a small number of "ignorant" or "redneck" whites who were racist. The emotions underlying these discourses included a desire for community, a fear of racial conflict, and a desire to maintain a positive self- and group image, which, students believed, was a precursor to racial harmony (i.e., if people of color saw only racism in white people, they would obviously not want to work toward interracial community). These desires were taught via emotioned rules embedded in multicultural lessons taught at Laurel Canyons.

Students often asserted that whites were the true or real victims of racial inequality in the United States. As Mike put it, "It's hard, when you're white. You don't get all the advantages." Michelle believed that whites had been overlooked: "It's like, look, my people have suffered too, and just because, like, we didn't have the Holocaust or slavery or whatever, it's not like it's been easy. My mom works really hard and she has suffered so my sister and me could have things. People don't realize that, but it's true. Whites don't have it easy, but like, you don't hear them complaining about it all the time." Laura believed that one of the lessons Angelou learns in her autobiography was to be "tolerant of white people." Students also believed that whites were victims of racism and that whites didn't get enough credit for enduring racism without complaint. They were quick, for example, to point out unfair generalizations about whites on the part of authors of color. "She [Angelou] totally stereotypes white people. Maybe some are like that, but not all," was a typical argument.

Interviews with students, however, revealed that these discourses—white victimhood, reverse racism—were rooted not so much in actual belief about race and racism but rather in students' desire for feelings of community and racial harmony, which were "emotioned positions" reinforced through multicultural lessons in the school. Texts that emphasized the social power whites possess or the oppression of people of color seemed to students to negate the possibility of racial harmony and community. If that's how they see us, students often told me, then "no wonder they hate us." Students could agree, when pushed, that whites had more advantages, but they didn't like admitting this because it appeared to negate the possibility of "getting along."

In contrast, claims of white victimhood and reverse racism were predicated on students' sense that making nonwhites understand their own, white, oppression was a strategy for creating common ground: "I just think, if they realized that whites have suffered too, maybe they would understand like, it is possible to just get over the race stuff and not be so mad all the time about it," Michelle said. Multicultural lessons taught in the school, as well as activities like the "multicultural club," which billed itself as creating cross-racial communities, structured these feelings by privileging tolerance and harmony, as well as equality and sameness, as important antiracist ideals.

Separating whites in terms of racist and nonracist, where "good" (i.e., middle-class) whites abhorred racism or practiced color blindness, was also a strategy that promoted students' sense of the possibility of interracial community. If racism could be located elsewhere, the path was cleared for "good" whites, as Laura positions herself in the transcript below, to "get along" with others regardless of race:

LAURA: I would never want to be part of that group [of redneck whites]. You can tell who they are in this school, like it's no secret who the hard workers and normal kids are and who the freaks are. Thank god.

JENNIFER: What would it be like, or what would you feel like, if you couldn't tell the difference? If it seemed like all white people were like the rednecks, or you couldn't tell who was who?

LAURA: I would not want to be associated with those people. It's like, I don't really know any Black people. But I read a lot of stuff by Blacks, like for school, so I know they think we're all a bunch of racist pigs. But if you look around here, you can see that's not true. We're not all like that. And if you want to know who the true racists are, they aren't hiding it, and it's not like you can say we're all like that. I'm sorry, most white people don't drive trucks and wear belt buckles and hick clothes and like have redneck Confederate flags in their windows. There are some kids like that here, but most definitely are not.

JENNIFER: What if it were true that African Americans thought all whites were racist? Why would that bother you? I'm not saying it shouldn't bother you; I'm just curious about how you think about it.

LAURA: I don't know. I guess it would be pretty upsetting to have everybody think you were a racist. Like if I was Black and I thought that, like, everyone was like the rednecks? All white people? I wouldn't even try the whole let's-just-get-along thing. I'd be all like, what's the point, they hate us, and like, I wouldn't blame them. I'd hate myself! . . . If Black people think that, why would they want to try to get along with us?

For Laura, to acknowledge racism was to give up on the "let's-just-get-along thing." Acknowledging racism threatened the possibility of interracial harmony and negated the positive feelings Laura derived from her desire to get along with others. Like Laura, Michelle also felt that without an acknowledgment that most whites weren't racist, interracial community would not be possible. Both students, in their efforts to preserve feelings of community, divided whites into "us/them" groups: "I just don't think you can say that. You know. Like if everybody felt that way, and it was like justified, I don't know, I think, like how would we ever move forward and like get over this race stuff? We'd be stuck. We'd always hate each other. I think like, there'd be no hope for like tolerance. Not to be all cheesy about it, but how would we ever start to get along?"

Feelings of racial harmony and community were set in linked opposition to one of the primary negative feelings associated with racism, shame, which was in turn linked to the social class divisions and aspirations of the school. Students often asserted common ground with people of color as a way of distancing themselves from the racism they associated with the "white trash" or "redneck" population of the school. Indeed, most students in the school agreed that racism was a problem only among a certain group of whites, those coming from working-class and rural backgrounds, some of whom did display Confederate flags in truck windows or even in school projects, as we saw with Josh, who used the Confederate flag in his identity poster. Middle-class identity at Laurel Canyons depended on cultivating an antiracist identity. Students like Laura adopted antiracist rhetoric as a way to acquire middle-class status and distinguish themselves from feelings of shame that arose from association with so-called rednecks and white trash. Locating racism elsewhere served two purposes for students: they could claim that they themselves were innocent of racism and simultaneously that they were victims of unfair stereotyping that painted all whites with the same brush. Students felt that these dual claims were important components of the goal of racial harmony.

The multiculturalism promoted in school practices such as the diversity club and lessons about tolerance and diversity supported students' sense that racism happened elsewhere, in other historically or socioeconomically distant groups of whites. The emotioned rules that gave reverse racism and white victimhood their persuasive force were located in multicultural lessons about interracial harmony, sameness, community, and ironically, antiracism. The ethos of "togetherness" was widely promoted throughout the school in multicultural lessons that bring people "of difference" together, as one student put it, and "show common ground."

"Anybody can make it if they try": Individualism

Many scholars have noted the tenacity of individualism—ideas such as anyone can make it, hard work leads inevitably to success, systemic injustices can be overcome by exertions of individual will—and the ways that the ideology of individualism promotes or legitimizes racism. Many students, for example, insisted that the "lesson" in each text, whether it explicitly addressed race or not, was about the centrality of individual will and individual hard work, and that such individual effort was the key to a successful life. They blamed hardship and struggle on individual lack of hard work and believed that every success was rooted in individual effort. This response was so pervasive that some students even managed to see *The Color Purple* as a morality tale about individual effort: As Michelle argued, the book showed the importance of learning proper English to "make something of yourself in life."

For students at Laurel Canyons, individualism was a way to enact powerful emotioned rules about strength and sameness or equality, rules that emerged at the school at least partly in response to social class inequality and were seen as a way to promote social cohesion among different groups of whites. Being strong and being the same as others were stressed particularly to mask or redirect attention from class difference and to diffuse conflict that arose from difference.

To see the complexity of students' investment in individualism, I want to take another look at Ashley's and Tori's responses to Angelou's *I Know Why the Caged Bird Sings*.

ASHLEY: [This book] is like, oh, you should feel sorry for us. And it's never going to be okay. But now they can go to school, and they aren't denied opportunities all the time. It's illegal now to deny them. So what more do they want? And [she's] like, it's never going to be okay, and I don't agree. It's illegal. Black people want us to get down on our knees. That's what I think. And I think [they] are trying to say white people are never going to be good enough, and we're better than you because of the past. The message I get from this book is it's white people's fault. It's like, oh, I'm going to whine about this and talk about everything that happened to me. It's race. She wants white people on their knees. It's like she's saying, "Look at me, cracker, you don't know my strength."

TORI: She like, gets her strength to put the blame on other people for like, her problems and stuff. But she doesn't realize how, like, that is not really going to work in the long run. It just weakens you if you like, blame people for your problems. You have to rely on yourself and be all like, it's up to you, if you want to succeed.

The immediate provocation for the discourse of individualism (Tori's comment that "you have to rely on yourself . . . if you want to succeed") is Ashley's assertion that Angelou is claiming superior strength and that Black people "want white people on their knees," a sentiment that, for Ashley and her peers, violated emotioned rules about being strong and "feeling equal" or the same. In Ashley's comments, whites were positioned defensively against a stronger, assertive racial "other." Raised here is the specter of whites as racially inferior but also, importantly, as weak. Weakness was associated throughout school culture with negative, highly discouraged behavior and attitudes. It was used to motivate students, much in the way it is often invoked in athletics. Students were often reminded that they needed to "be strong" and "buck up." Behavior such as fighting, not doing homework, having a bad attitude toward school, not participating in school, was often labeled by both students and teachers as weak. "You're never going to make it if you just give up. That's weak," was a common refrain. When texts emphasized power struggles between racial groups, students dismissed characters they deemed weak or employed discourses of individualism to imbue the characters with strength.

In addition, reminders of difference of any kind violated what Ashley called a "feeling of equality" that students valued as integral to social cohesion. "I think, like if you want to be friends and have all the groups at this school get along, you have to understand that we're all equal, and just because someone might have more money than you or wear different clothes, it doesn't mean we're not equal." Ashley went on to talk about how her family's hard work had closed the gap between her economic situation and that of many of her classmates': "Maybe my family doesn't have as much money as like some of the kids around here. But my dad works really hard, and like my brother and me, we have jobs that pay for like school clothes. So you can't really say that we're not equal." Discourses of individualism—ideas such as "anybody can make it"—restored an important balance of power and masked social class differences. When reminders of power differences came in the form of an author, like Angelou, who pointed out racism, Ashley and her peers felt that the "feeling of equality" was being compromised.

The emotioned appeals to equality were taught via several tacit aspects of the school's pedagogy and philosophy, particularly its stance toward the working-class, rural students who attended Laurel Canyons. Part of the principal's mission was to help the bottom socioeconomic tier achieve middle-class status, and this meant, as he said, raising expectations and changing habits and values, making students and their families see the importance of those aspects of Laurel Canyons' curriculum that were particularly geared toward an elite education. "We want everyone here to feel like they can make it," the principal said in an interview. The school's open tracking system, allowing any student to take any class, was also part of its effort to promote equality. "No one here needs to feel like anyone is better than anyone else. If you want to, if you work hard, you can achieve in any class you take."

The emotions underlying the discourses I've been analyzing here and the school practices that shaped and gave rise to those emotions are not structured neatly together. As Lindquist (2002) writes, such discourses are not like puzzle pieces that fit along the same plane to make a coherent picture. Discourses, emotions, school practices, and values do not operate "relationally or chronologically or linearly; they were, rather, points of entry into the textured densities of ideology" (Lindquist 74). Individualism and instrumentalism, reverse racism and desires for community, white innocence and the importance of a positive attitude were embedded together in complex ways. They were interconnected and emotioned strands of discourse that derived from school practices and were constitutive of a tacitly racialized emotioned universe.

White Superiority and Biological Explanations of Race

Two of the most stridently racist discourses that I encountered as I observed Elizabeth's classes were white superiority and biological explanations of racial difference. Although they did so cautiously, and sometimes in hushed whispers that suggested an understanding of the taboo nature of what they were saying, students sometimes asserted that whites were superior to other racial groups and that racial difference could be explained by way of biology and genetics. When confronted with texts that challenged racism, students sometimes countered by claiming that whites were genetically or biologically inclined to work harder, care about school, value family, know how to get ahead, avoid crime, and know how to raise children.

In the following transcript, Mike, Tom, and James digressed from a discussion of *The Color Purple* (their assigned small-group task) to a broader discussion of contemporary race relations and the differences between whites and Blacks.

Tom: It's a fact that like, they're better at sports but not at school. Like, they're not as smart, testwise or whatever, and that's a fact, and like no one will admit it, but it's totally true.

James: What do you mean that it's like a fact? I know the sports thing. Like just look around and it's obvious that they kick our ass at sports. It's genetic. But you can't prove, like, they aren't as smart.

Mike: Dude, it's as obvious as the sports thing. Do you see them like striving in society, getting ahead?

Tom: You can prove it with statistics about IQ tests and like, SAT scores. I heard it on the radio. Their scores are lower, like regardless of racism, you can't say, oh, it's racism that makes it so I can't like, score high on a test. So, it's a fact.

Mike [turning to me]: I have no idea what radio station he listens to. What like, the Ku Klux Klan morning show?

Jennifer: So you disagree with him?

Mike: You can't argue with facts. You heard him, it's a statistic. It shows they aren't as smart as white people.

Discourses that asserted unchanging and invidious cultural, as opposed to biological, differences were also prevalent, particularly among those students who didn't want to appear racist. Invoking biological difference was understood as racist; making negative claims about different cultures was sometimes framed as open-mindedness, as we'll see below. In this transcript, Laura and Alicia are discussing whether Laurel Canyons students were racist.

LAURA: Kids will say stuff, but they don't mean it, or they've had a bad experience that like, you know, makes them feel that way, or like I don't know, sometimes, if like something is true, because of a person's culture, and you might not like that, then you're not being racist against a race, just against certain things that some cultures do. I don't think there's anything wrong with that.

ALICIA: My dad's like that. He's had a lot of experience with Black people, like at his work, and he says its not because they're Black but just like, what they value in their culture is not what we value. And my dad's like, it's not racist to say that somebody's values disagree with yours.

JENNIFER: Can you give an example of values that disagree with yours?

LAURA: Yeah, like you see it at this school, with the rednecks. Like it's not race, but I don't want to be like them, like all not trying and make something of yourself. And a lot of Black people, not all, but a lot, are like, we don't want to work hard, we just want handouts, and like to me, it's not racist to disagree with that.

ALICIA: It's just their culture that like, it doesn't value the value of hard work and trying to better yourself. A lot of them just learn, like from their parents, that it's okay to be lazy and just let other people take care of you.

Several days after the exchange above, I asked Laura to revisit her comments about her father's assessment of African American cultural values and to contemplate a different explanation for the poverty that plagues people of color disproportionately in the United States.

JENNIFER: I know you were saying a few weeks ago, when we were talking, that you and your dad felt like certain races have cultural values like "it's okay to be lazy" and "let other people take care of you." Is that right? Am I getting it right?

LAURA: Yeah, like it's not like racist if you can say, look, I disagree with this culture, that just like wants to be lazy. You're not saying, like black people are all lazy or something. But certain cultures, even with white people, but a lot with black cultures, and Indians, or Native Americans or whatever, just want a handout. Even some white people are like that.

JENNIFER: What would you say if, actually, that wasn't accurate, but instead, like, the reason you sometimes see people of color needing assistance from the government is that racism has made it impossible for them to thrive, so it's not that their culture encourages laziness but rather that American culture, even white culture, has made it impossible for their hard work to pay off. What if that were true, how would you feel?

LAURA: Well, okay, but like, you can't blame your problems on other people. That's what I was always taught, and like, even if it is someone else's fault, you have to take responsibility because like, you're the only one who can take responsibility for your life, you know?

JENNIFER: What if you could, even sometimes maybe you should, blame other people because those other people, in this case, white people, need to take responsibility for what they've done? So what if, let's say, it actually was good to sometimes try to get other people, who really are at fault, to take responsibility for the problems they've caused?

LAURA: You can't blame problems on other people.

JENNIFER: Even if these other people actually caused the problem?

LAURA: Okay, if you want, like, it's okay for everyone to do that? If everybody did that? You'd end up like Holden Caulfield. Totally crazy and like depressed because no one wants to be around someone who just whines all the time and wants other people to solve their problems. And it's like, I've heard it enough times from like parents and teachers and coaches, that you can't blame other people and if you do, you're just this pathetic person who is totally like, unable to be functional or get anywhere in life. And then like, if everyone was like that? It'd be chaos, and like, really ugly, because who would ever get anything done? It'd all just be, like, me me me, instead of like, look we all have to like suffer at some point. Everyone has some problems that hold them back.

In her answers to my questions, Laura avoided the topic of race altogether, even citing a white male character, Holden Caulfield of *Catcher in the Rye*, as an example of the negative traits she associated with people of color. One way to interpret this avoidance is through the lens of contemporary antiracist pedagogy: Laura avoids because she doesn't want to confront her own racism or her complicity in systemic causes of inequality and injustice. But to accept this interpretation, we have to ignore several interesting features of Laura's responses: We have to ignore Laura's reiteration of a value constantly taught in school—the idea of taking responsibility and being responsible—her reference to a white character (Holden Caulfield) whom Laura judged as harshly as, if not more harshly than, she did Angelou; the similarities between her response to Holden Caulfield and her beliefs about "certain" cultures; and her sense that a different framing—one that allowed and encouraged people to assign blame where it was due and to critique systems rather than individuals—would lead not to social change that might cause a loss of her own social privilege but to weakness ("you're just this pathetic person") and the breakdown of social life ("It'd be chaos"). The threat of personal weakness that Laura cites was, as we've seen, a powerful emotioned rule taught in a variety of contexts through the school. The fear of loss of control, either personal or social, was also part of the school's emotioned universe. Indeed, it is interesting to note that in another conversation with Tom, he said that listening to right-wing talk radio helped him feel like the world made sense, and kept confusion and loss of epistemological control at bay: "It, like, kind of simplifies things, but in a good way, so you know what to think and how to understand stuff. Like the whole race thing, they make it easier to understand, and I think that's good because part of the problem is, like, all this disagreement and arguing is just craziness and makes everybody crazy because they don't know what to think or who to believe." Much of the institutional life of Laurel Canyons might be said to function similarly: managing what might appear as chaotic or conflicting social relations through simplifying practices like moving between classes only when bells ring, assigning letter grades to students, counting words in journal entries, et cetera. Even Elizabeth acknowledged that without the control such routines introduced, chaos would reign. "Hey, everybody, it's not a free-for-all," she would say when the noise reached a certain pitch in class. "Let's sit down, read the instructions, and do the work. If everybody just follows their own rules, we'll never get through this." Julie, the inclusion teacher, once remarked to me that the main purpose of her job was to manage students and "keep the chaos at bay."

This focus on order and control undergirded many students' most racist proclamation. Discourses about unchanging differences between groups served to manage what appeared to students to be overwhelming complexity, which in turn threatened to spill over into social chaos. Tracing these discourses makes clear that addressing Laura's racism with multicultural antidotes—exposure to difference, the cultivation of empathy for others—or with the stronger medicine of interrogating whiteness and privilege will miss the mark. Instead, we need attention to the ways school practices teach emotions that structure students' responses to matters of race.

Conclusion

The connections between society's hierarchical socioeconomic structure and schooling, which often mirrors the social structure, is well known. Study after study has shown how schools both promote and reinforce social class hierarchies and identities through taken-for-granted practices. These studies focus on the institutional and pedagogical—how students are tracked, how classroom participation structures are organized, how classroom practices uphold and teach class subjectivity, how teachers uphold class-based ideologies in their interactions with students. The focus of these studies is institutional: they are about how institutions promote and legitimize hierarchical social relations. But studies of race and schooling have been oddly private, as scholars have asked less institutional and more private questions: how might a particular curriculum get white students to see the world in new ways, to give up old views and beliefs? This scholarship tends to focus on the curriculum (are people of color adequately represented?) and on changing individual student consciousness, making students more empathetic, more tolerant of difference, less ignorant of others, more aware of white privilege. In this way, antiracist educators have seemed to start at the end—with assumptions that a racist utterance means a racist student who will perpetuate racism unless his education intervenes first—and project into the future: how can teachers accomplish, next time or later in the term, the requisite psychological adjustment that, it is hoped, will occur between a teacher or text and a student, creating that elusive transformation from ignorance or self-interest in matters of race to an "antiracist" consciousness? At the same time, paradoxically, students' responses to these efforts at individual transformation have been understood in almost exclusively political terms, as evidence of the student's location in matrices of privilege, and as proof of his or her ideological beliefs.

What I've tried to suggest instead is the need to interpret students differently, to examine racism not as an individual failing that occurs in isolated moments in the classroom, or as a manifestation in the student of flaws in the political order (where the student is seen as mouthing the racist logic of his or her culture). Instead, we need to see student racism as a mediated emotioned phenomenon that emerges from and responds to the routines and culture of schooling. Such analysis moves differently across time and collapses the distinction between public and private that structure many interpretations of students.

Lindquist (2004) writes that we must "mak[e] room for the products of students' emotional labor in scenes of literacy instruction" and notes that we need more attention to "the pedagogical work of emotion"—understood as both a private and public phenomenon—in the classroom. The challenges inherent in this shift in perspective are the subject of the next chapter, where I describe in more detail Elizabeth's commitment to critical pedagogy and antiracism and examine the contradictory emotioned rules at play within these pedagogical traditions. The shift Lindquist calls for will require that we pay attention to the ways that schools themselves structure the emotional ideals that students internalize. The emotioned rules I've examined here are embedded in almost every aspect of school culture, from sports activities to hall passes to grading and authority relations. Researchers have long articulated the ways that aspects of schooling teach social class subjectivity. But we also need to understand how schooling contributes to the system of racism that students' discourses about race help to support. Ultimately, understanding these discourses and their relation to the world of emotions and to the institutional structures that govern students' lives might allow us to create rhetorics of social change that persuade.

4

WHEN TO BREAK THE RULES
FEBRUARY, MARCH, AND APRIL

> Teaching, like research, involves situated readings of students.
> —Deborah Hicks, *Reading Lives*

An easy pitfall in ethnographic writing about education is the construction of teacher-heroes or teacher-scapegoats, characterizations of teachers as the source of or the solution to problems such as those we have seen in chapter 3. In struggling to avoid this pitfall, I have come to see the importance of blurring the usual lines separating the teacher from the researcher or from the audience, lines that position Elizabeth as the subject of analysis while I retain the power of representation. Such lines engender easy narratives, their familiarity and comfort either allowing us to feel that the intractable racism chronicled throughout this book is the product of Elizabeth's missteps or misguided pedagogy or providing us with a reassuring teacher-hero whose pedagogical moves successfully transformed her students and who provides us with a model to emulate in our own classrooms. Elizabeth did not fit neatly into either of these narratives.

To fully account for Elizabeth's teaching without making her the object of my gaze is a seemingly impossible contradiction. Even so, I attempt to navigate the impossible in the following pages by breaking down the distinction between the observed and the observer. This chapter, which focuses on how an incomplete engagement with the emotioned rules embedded in her teaching stymied Elizabeth's efforts to enact a successful antiracist pedagogy, blurs the lines between researcher and researched, as I emphasize how *both* Elizabeth and I, in our responses to students, in our characterizations of them, and in our pedagogical and political commitments, were hindered by a lack of understanding of the affective dimensions of education—the emotioned rules at play in school—and how these rules shaped students' responses to race. To blur the lines between Elizabeth and me, I highlight the interconnectedness of our stories, the similarities between us. Narratives and transcripts in this chapter foreground our relationship, illustrate my interactions with students, as well as hers, and describe the collaboration that emerged between us as the year progressed. In turning the gaze on her, I thus turn it more fully on myself.

Indeed, I chose to work with Elizabeth because she reflected my own values more fully than any of the other teachers I interviewed or observed. In that sense, her story is my story, and the story of her classroom is the story of my experiences as a researcher in her classroom. In my representation of the shortcomings in Elizabeth's pedagogy, I focus on those that I share with her—blind spots that were revealed to me only in the luxury of hindsight, as I sifted through my notes and transcripts months and years later. Shortcomings that were specific to Elizabeth—her tendency toward indirection in the classroom as she struggled to enact a truly student-centered pedagogy, her occasional flashes of impatience and frustration—I have chosen to downplay or omit out of respect for her and a desire to honor her generosity in sharing her classroom with me for an entire year. But I also downplay her individual shortcomings as a teacher because, having completed my analysis of the ethnographic materials I gathered, I want to emphasize that Elizabeth cannot be understood as the source of or the sole solution to the problems described here.

I met Elizabeth when I was directing the local Writing Project's Summer Institute for Teachers. For several months I had been looking for a teacher to participate in my study: I needed someone who taught in a predominantly white high school and who instructed in a critically minded way, that is, she or he would address students' thinking about matters of race and identity and would engage students in reading, writing, and talking about matters of social justice. When the interviewing for the Summer Institute began, I had already chased a number of promising leads: teachers were recommended to me by other Writing Project members, and I visited schools and classrooms and conducted e-mail and phone conversations with prospective teachers. Most of these teachers, though committed in general to helping students become more open-minded and tolerant, saw multiculturalism either as an opportunity to teach white students that "race doesn't matter" or as a chance to provide them with examples of uplift and progress. Some teachers talked about their desire to protect white students' innocence by not exposing them to the harsh realities of race and injustice; others wanted to motivate students to work hard and believe in themselves, and they saw multicultural texts about overcoming obstacles as central to this goal. One teacher I interviewed did try to challenge her students to interrogate race (for example, asking them to predict the race of various characters, solely on the basis of paragraph-length descriptions of them, and using students' predictions to talk about stereotypes), but she was leaving for a sabbatical and would have been available for only half the year. Other teachers I spoke to were unaware of the literature on critical pedagogy or antiracism, or had actively rejected it as not appropriate for their students or school. Most of the teachers I worked with in the Summer Institute gave similar descriptions of their teaching philosophy and practice: they were committed to helping students get past negative stereotypes and learn to be tolerant of others, and they believed they could best accomplish this goal by teaching students that we're all the same on the inside, that difference didn't matter.

Elizabeth was different. During the initial interview for the Writing Project Summer Institute, she spoke often about her struggle to get her students to view the world with a skeptical eye, to become aware of and concerned about injustices of all kinds. Asked about her most important goal as a teacher, she talked about motivating students to leave the "bubble" of their protected suburban existence and the comfortable political discourses that sustained it. She wanted to challenge her students to think critically about social issues and to reflect on their worlds and identities. A risk taker who wasn't afraid to challenge students, parents, or administrators, she was passionate about politics and deeply engaged by many of the questions that motivated my own work on whiteness, racism, and pedagogy. When we began to plan her participation in my study, I visited her classroom and saw bulletin boards displaying political cartoons and announcements of poetry readings, art exhibits, and films. She showed me the curricular guides for Advanced Writing and Introduction to Humanities, which she had helped write, and I saw a curriculum that deftly satisfied district requirements while also challenging students to consider issues of identity, language, and power—to "go beyond easy answers," as Elizabeth often put it. She talked about the texts and teachers that had influenced her: Paulo Freire, bell hooks, *Ways of Reading*, and her own experience in a first-year composition course in college, where she had a dedicated teacher who took her, line by line, through her own writing, showing her the power of carefully chosen words and introducing her to the pleasures of intellectual work, as well as the ideas she discovered in later courses in gender, film, and multicultural literatures. She returned again and again to *Ways of Reading*, which she first encountered in her composition class as a freshman and then rediscovered in her teaching credential program. Although *Ways of Reading* is not generally aimed at critical teachers—it is not overtly political in its approach—for Elizabeth, it contained a powerful message at its center that aligned with her goals as a critical teacher: the student is at the center of the pedagogical process and is empowered to be—indeed must become—an intellectual. Being an intellectual, for Elizabeth, was synonymous with a politics of social justice and change, and with antiracism. She believed that it was her job as an English teacher to teach students how to pay attention to language—their own and that of others—and to show them the relationship between language and ways of living in and understanding the larger social world. As she put it, "I really believe that it's by learning to read and write critically that you start to question things, and it's that questioning spirit that leads you to challenge inequality or racism. For me, teaching against racism starts with teaching critical reading and writing." But like so many of us who enter the classroom armed with theories of social change through literacy education, Elizabeth often encountered resistant students and what Ira Shor calls the disabling routines of institutional practice. In the rest of this chapter, which again relies on mixed genres—narrative and more traditional ethnographic analysis—I examine the emotioned rules at work in Elizabeth's antiracist pedagogy and the ways those rules framed students' rhetorical positions on matters of race.

In the rest of this chapter, which again relies on mixed genres—narrative and more traditional ethnographic analysis—I examine the emotioned rules at work in Elizabeth's antiracist pedagogy and the ways those rules framed students' rhetorical positions on matters of race.

In Advanced Writing that winter, the students began a unit on poetry. Elizabeth gave them thick packets of photocopied poems by local writers. Some were from *The Dig* by Lynn Emmanuel. Others were from a book called *Postmortem* by Maurice Kilwein-Guevara. There was also a collection from Amish writer Julia Kasdorf, as well as poems and an essay—"When We Dead Awaken"—by Adrienne Rich. The first assignment was for students to skim through the packets, reading any poem that intrigued them. To kick off discussion, students would read out loud one poem or a section from a poem that interested them and then say a few words about why they chose it. The final assignment, which Elizabeth and I worked on together, asked students first to analyze assumptions that made their reading of a particular poem difficult and then to try their hand at writing a poem themselves.

Laura hated all the poems and was absent on the poetry-reading day. "I think she picks the hardest poems on purpose to frustrate us," she said of Elizabeth. She was angry about her midterm grade. "If my best isn't good enough," she said the day after getting her midterm portfolio back, "then I'm not sure what I'm supposed to do. It's just another example of how hard work doesn't pay off at this school, and that's not how it's supposed to be."

"Did you see we have to write our own poem for part two of this assignment?" Jessica asked.

"Just write something dumb and confusing, and she'll think it's brilliant," Laura said. "If we look at these poems, then all we have to do is write a poem that makes no sense at all."

"I'm not sure what the purpose of that would be," Elizabeth responded from across the room. She was in Jacob and Rich's group, trying to get them to analyze the language of the poem rather than evaluate the psychological state of the writer. "You can't just say she was neglected as a child, and that's why she writes about this stuff. You've got to stick to the text, not just what is being said but how it's being said. Like think about Angelou and how she said things in ways that made us respond a certain way. And when we heard the same ideas from Wideman, who said them differently and made different choices as a writer, he got different responses. So we need to look not just at what she's saying but how she's saying it in the choices she's making as a writer."

"I hate poetry."

"Especially these poems!" Laura said. "They're all just a bunch of white trash people. Motels and prostitutes and cigarettes. It's disgusting." She was referring to some of Emmanuel's poems.

"When I read them, it was like Charlie Brown's teacher talking!" Tori said.

"I only like poetry when it rhymes," another student said.

"I'm not smart enough for poetry."

Elizabeth posted an announcement about an upcoming poetry reading at a local university campus.

"God help me if I ever go to a poetry reading," Laura muttered loudly.

"Okay, maybe we need to deal with our feelings about poetry before we can do this!" Elizabeth said.

"I really hate it."

"It makes everything so complicated. I read it, and I'm like, what is the big deal?"

"And also," Heather began, "like, I don't understand. Everyone has a different opinion, and yet there's a right answer or else how would she grade us? Especially with poetry, it's just your interpretation. You can't say if it's right or wrong."

"Yeah," Laura said. "Like if I'm happy looking at one side of things, that should be enough."

The discussion continued, wandering into specific complaints about the readings, particularly the poems by Rich and Emmanuel.

"Feminists are annoying, like the stupid ACLU people?" Laura said about Rich. "Like our rights are being trampled. Just because you're a woman. I think it's ridiculous. Just do the work and stop complaining about everything. Every time I see something about feminists, I just refuse to read it. I don't agree with it, and I don't want to read it because I don't agree with it."

"Ditto," Rich said. "I don't care about the reading when it's by people I don't like, like feminists and stuff. This assignment meant nothing to me."

"I related better to Emmanuel because she was positive. [Adrienne] Rich was too negative. I couldn't relate."

"I'll play devil's advocate for a minute," Elizabeth said, as she made her rounds past each group. "Yes, Rich is a difficult text, maybe harder for you to understand than Emmanuel's because of the references and because it's so much a product of its time. But what does that mean you do as a reader? Just throw up your hands?"

"It's her responsibility to make us understand."

"What about our responsibilities as readers?" Elizabeth countered.

"Why would you take any responsibility for understanding something you hate?"

"Because how can you hate it when you don't understand it?"

"It's just like everything else, extreme feminism. The general message is just, men are bad."

"A long time ago, I could see the need for feminism, but not now."

"Women still only make seventy-five cents to the dollar," I said.

"Yeah, but maybe it's because they want to raise families or something."

"I think even if you disagree with it, you should still read it and try to understand. I mean if you refuse to read everything you disagree with you can't really learn anything or like, grow as a person. You can't know what you believe if you don't know what others think," Jessica said. She loved Elizabeth's class and often tried to diffuse her peers' resistance.

"But you shouldn't let other people influence your views."

"Plus, this is like, just hard to read. She's yelling at everyone. It's unrealistic. Women are 50 percent of the population. It's not like you're outnumbered if you really wanted to change things. If you' re so mad, go do something about it and stop complaining."

"She's very militant," another student added. "She generalizes against men."

"I thought it was funny that she claimed to be this big feminist but she was married and had three kids."

"Why is that funny?" I asked.

"Because feminists are lesbians. She seems to have forgotten that."

"The problem is her extreme feminism," Laura said. "She said the same points as Emmanuel but then like turned it into a feminist thing. I studied feminism last year, and I hated it."

That night, Laura wrote in a journal entry, "I think Adrienne is an extreme feminist who's [sic] radical views about the oppression of women have influenced how she sees the writing process. Her whole point is that women need to work so much harder just to equal men or even just to get our works studied. But she overstates it. She gets too worked up. It's like, chill out."

Later that week, Elizabeth and I talked about the frustrating contradictions we experienced in our efforts to enact antiracist and critical education. We wanted to empower the students and to honor their points of view. Elizabeth said, "I was their age once. I didn't always have a great perspective on these issues, like racism." But we also wanted to change the students, to make them believe differently, and I include myself in this sentence because by this point in the year, Elizabeth's struggles with the students in Advanced Writing and Introduction to Humanities had become my own. We often discussed the students together during her planning period, and I worked hard with Elizabeth to come up with strategies and activities that were designed to achieve her goals. We both agreed that the students' positions on most social issues were scary. Laura was one of several students in the class who became "go-to" examples of the difficulties of critical teaching. Indeed, Elizabeth and I spoke of these students often: they were hopeless, we said, and we cited them frequently in our conversations about the challenges of critical teaching at Laurel Canyons. Two students also became, for a month or so that year, the source of much teacherly angst on Elizabeth's part, as they responded with barely concealed resentment to their midterm grades and refused, for a few weeks, to participate in class at all. Indeed, our feelings about these students were so strong that Elizabeth made them central characters in a teaching demonstration she developed for the Writing Project the following summer, using Plato's Allegory of the Cave to describe student resistance. "What about students who refuse to learn?" Elizabeth asked during her presentation. "What about students who don't want to come out of the cave?"

Laura was a particularly frustrating case. "She makes sure everything is by the book—never misses an assignment, follows directions to the letter, wouldn't break a rule if her life depended on it, but somehow she still manages to miss the whole point of what we're trying to do," I said to Elizabeth after class one day. It was snowing and gray outside. We sat in the classroom; the Advanced Writing students had just filed out, leaving a trailing silence in their wake. Laura and several other students were angry about their grades. As Laura said, she had "followed all the rules on every assignment" but "it still wasn't good enough." Looking back on Laura's work in Elizabeth's class, it seems now that what made Laura an especially hopeless case to Elizabeth and me was just this: her paradoxical relationship to rules. She was zealous about following them and adroit in enacting them, but somehow she still managed to avoid engaging with the larger ideas that Elizabeth was trying to teach. She had perfected the arts of resistance: she managed to resist authority and avoid certain kinds of learning without ever appearing to violate a rule.

Elizabeth's and my sense of Laura as hopeless is an example of what Deborah Hicks calls a "situated reading" of a student, one marked by a kind of "critical illiteracy," which Min Zhan Lu (1998) defines as moments when teachers fail to manifest their own critical goals. In the rest of this chapter, I extend Lu's term from teacher practice to teacher *and researcher* practice in an exploration of how Elizabeth and I constructed situated readings of students that limited our ability to address them persuasively. I also extend the term *critical illiteracy* to the rhetoric of antiracist pedagogy that informed our practice. This rhetoric sometimes disabled students' engagement with antiracist ideas in Elizabeth's classroom because of its incomplete engagement with the affective rules embedded in it. As I use the term, *critical illiteracy* refers to classroom rhetorical practices, along with the research and theory that undergird them, that aim toward antiracist pedagogical goals but that inadvertently reinforce or scaffold racist discourses or practices. In chapter 3, many aspects of schooling at Laurel Canyons enforced emotioned rules that in their application or enactment, made racism persuasive. This chapter shows how aspects of critical and antiracist teaching also tacitly and inadvertently promoted emotioned rules that gave rise to racism or that stymied students' engagement with antiracism. At the end of the chapter is a discussion of moments in Elizabeth's classroom when students productively navigated the contradictions embedded in the emotioned rules at play at Laurel Canyons and in Elizabeth's classroom. Such moments return us to a central theme of this book: time and its relationship to learning and to representation.

While the focus here is on the emotional rules embedded (and sometimes explicitly taught) in practices of critical pedagogy and antiracist education, also important is the tacit articulation of these rules in the literature on antiracist education. These rules sometimes disable the goals of critical education, in part because they clash with the schoolwide emotioned rules described in chapter 3 but also because antiracist education has not sufficiently accounted for the dynamics of emotion in the context of schooling. Boler (1999) has written about how multicultural education enforces emotional control through its emphasis on empathy. Others have written about the role of shame and guilt in antiracist education, but few have examined the ways in which rules about empathy, shame, and guilt are actually taught. Thus, this chapter argues that we must attend to the emotioned rules that are—intentionally or not—taught via antiracist education and the way these rules sometimes hinder antiracist goals.

In analyzing Elizabeth's and my interactions with Laura, I noticed again and again the kinds of critical illiteracy Lu describes, particularly in our lack of awareness of the ways that critical pedagogy sets up conflicting emotioned rules for students like her. For example, Elizabeth and I ignored, even as we deplored, the affective dimensions of Laura's participation in class and her response to Elizabeth's teaching, and we failed to understand the contradictory emotioned rules Laura navigated as a student. These failures, I want to suggest, are not ours alone. They are built into the rhetoric of antiracist teaching.

The emotion-based rules embedded in Elizabeth's teaching may be traced to values and emotions implicit in antiracist education and to the wider school practices chronicled in the previous chapter. If students' racism is upheld and even promoted by emotioned rules not always related to race, teachers' efforts to change students' ideas about race are similarly hamstrung. We end up promoting critically illiterate perspectives and practices because of our own incomplete engagement with the ways emotioned rules work in the context of critical pedagogical persuasion.

Learning How to Feel about Race

One of the feelings taught in Elizabeth's class was a sense of satisfaction and even superiority that came from opposing racism and oppression. Those who aligned themselves openly with racism were labeled "rednecks" and "white trash," and as we have seen, students like Laura carefully delineated herself from such students, often using antiracist rhetoric to do so. Elizabeth encouraged students to draw moral lines between racists and their victims and to side with and empathize with victims of injustice, and she modeled this line-drawing in class. She argued passionately for justice during class discussions, making it clear that she had little patience for those who perpetrated injustice of any kind. She invited students to share her outrage.

But at the same time, impassioned moral outrage—which calls for a judgmental stance, as well as for feelings of certainty—often conflicted with the practices of tolerance, open-mindedness, and self-critique that antiracist education demands and that Elizabeth emphasized. Tolerance and open-mindedness were, in fact, widely held values at Laurel Canyons: being close-minded was one step above being racist, in many students' minds, and racism was deeply associated with negative feelings of shame, as well as with disgust for socioeconomically "othered" groups of whites. "Rednecks" and "white trash" were thought to be racist and were contrasted with middle-class whites who understood that racism was wrong. Both Laura and Ashley worked hard in their responses to texts to avoid appearing racist or close-minded. Both indicated that appearing to be racist caused deep anxiety about their identity as part of the middle class. For Laura, being close-minded threatened her status as one of the "normal" kids in school. She did not want to be associated with rednecks. Much of her responses to texts was the result of this fear, which was promoted throughout the peer culture of Laurel Canyons. (Almost every student I asked about racism at Laurel Canyons claimed that the only students who were racist were the rednecks.) Teachers echoed this view, according to Elizabeth. Her colleagues, she said, did not see racism unless there was a kid with a Confederate flag on his locker. In this way, students and teachers could demonstrate both their outrage at racism and simultaneously assert, via their proclaimed distance from it, their own open-minded tolerance of different races.

In the following transcript, students in Elizabeth's Advanced Writing class were discussing Rich's "When We Dead Awaken: Writing as ReVision." The students recognized the ethical line-drawing that Rich, in her critique of patriarchy, is engaged in, but they struggled to determine who is on which side of these lines, a struggle made more complicated by their awareness of the need for "tolerance."

TORI: I'm female, and this essay, it just makes you think, like about how men had all the control of things in our society. And its like, thank god things are equal now.

ASHLEY: But it's not like, men, you know, they aren't like the Ku Klux Klan where you can just say, okay, like these guys are against women and we need to fight against them and be all, against them. It's like, who is suppressing women? There isn't a group, and you can't say all men are like that. Like that would make us as bad as them, if we were just all stereotyping men.

TORI: So it's like, yeah, in this story, what is she really talking about in this story. I mean, women should be equal and all that, and I don't agree with the past, how women were forced to stay at home and couldn't vote and all. But now, I'm not sure it's an issue anymore.

ASHLEY: Sometimes my dad is like, really sexist, but I'm not going to criticize him! He's my dad! And he doesn't mean anything by it, you know?

One of the most salient features of this transcript is the way the students appear to deny or rationalize sexism, first in Tori's assertion that it isn't "an issue anymore" and then in Ashley's unwillingness to critique her father's sexism ("he doesn't mean anything by it"). But what seems to give rise to the students' rationalization is the difficulty they have in practicing tolerance and avoiding the stereotyping they are trying to critique, while at the same time drawing clear ethical lines that position "sexists" on one side and women on the other. As Ashley says, "there isn't a group, and you can't say all men are like that," suggesting the difficulty students faced as they tried to feel both outraged at sexism and tolerant of all groups at the same time.

Students feared being caught on the wrong side of the lines that antiracism and multiculturalism drew, and as a result, they overextended the rules of tolerance. Sometimes there was a sly, even subversive knowingness to this, as we saw in the previous chapter, when a student questioned the fairness of "discriminating" against those who preferred not to think deeply. At other times, students seemed to make an effort to be open-minded and tolerant but did so about issues that were, in the moral universe of Elizabeth's classroom, not actually tolerated, as above when the students make an effort to be open-minded about sexism ("you can't say all men are like that"). Students worked hard to establish themselves on the side of justice: "I don't want to be one of those people who just stereotypes people and can't think for yourself," Ashley said during an interview. "If I was like, close-minded," she continued, "I would not be very happy with myself. I don't think like racist people can feel much good about themselves. Like, look in the mirror. But they probably don't want to." But the stigma attached to being close-minded sometimes translated into an unwillingness to call anything into question, as we see above in the students' discussion of sexism. Many students did not want to appear to stereotype any group—including men, whites, the wealthy—and so were confused by discussion in which interrogation of the practices and attitudes or language of particular groups was demanded.

As Virginia Anderson argues, confusion about inclusion and exclusion, tolerance and difference, saturates critical discourse. On one hand, critical perspectives promote a kind of moral exclusivity, constructing lines between "us" as enlightened and right-minded and "them" as perpetuating injustice. A commitment to social justice, Anderson argues, necessitates such moral boundary drawing. But this necessity contradicts an equally important commitment to tolerance and acceptance of difference. As a result, we teach students to feel negatively toward racism and positively toward a harmonious inclusiveness, while at the same time we insist that they practice moral line-drawing that makes clear distinctions between those on the side of justice and those who perpetuate injustice.

Similar conflicting emotioned rules came into play during discussions of cultural or racial difference. Difference, at Laurel Canyons, was generally felt to be dangerous. It was associated, in official school discourses, with conflict. When a conflict occurred between students or between a teacher and student, school officials often cast it as resulting from a failure to see commonality, from too much emphasis on difference. "Just because someone doesn't dress like you or talk like you or come from the same neighborhood as you doesn't mean you can't relate to them," Julie, the inclusion teacher said one day to a group of boys who were recounting a confrontation that had taken place after a football game. "You probably have more in common than you think." Students were taught that the way to avoid conflict was to value equality and to view everyone as equal. The school's open-tracking policy was one of the ways it promoted what Ashley called "a feeling of equality": "I like the way you can take whatever you want, like hard classes or easy classes, and just mix with whatever group you want. There's a feeling of equality at this school and like that helps people get along, even if there are, you know, some people are really popular or some are not or whatever. There's still a feeling of equality, and that would like help with racism too. When there are other races at this school, it's like there's not very many of them, but they can mix in with everyone else because we're all equal."

Students were often exhorted to remember that everyone was equal. As one administrator told me, "we work hard to make sure that everyone understands the importance of equality and respect, that the kids don't think somebody's better than somebody else or worse than somebody else, just because they're different. Everyone is equal, and understanding that is important for promoting tolerance and helping the students get along with different groups."

However, recognizing inequality and valuing difference were promoted in Elizabeth's class. This emphasis confused students, who had been trained elsewhere in school to ignore inequality and difference in favor of sameness. Students applied the emotioned rule to feel equal to many other social and pedagogical contexts. They were quick to point out other students who "thought they were better than everybody," and they similarly resented authors or characters who pointed out or highlighted difference. They were confused by Elizabeth's attempts to explore differences: for students, such an exploration was an invitation to conflict. "You can't have people saying, 'I'm so different, I'm so special,' and then expect everyone to be equal," Laura pointed out. "I think everyone's the same on the inside, or else how would we have ended racism in the first place? Like if they hadn't seen that slaves were like, basically just like everybody else?"

When confronted with racial difference in the texts they read, students often continued to apply this rule, dismissing characters or authors who violated the "feeling of equality" that they felt was central to getting along, and celebrating authors whom they interpreted as promoting a feeling of equality. The transcript below is illustrative. Students are discussing John Edgar Wideman's "Our Time," from *Brothers and Keepers*:

LAURA: I like John a lot because he's like, humble about his accomplishments and doesn't make you feel bad because he's had it so hard, even though he did not have a good, or like wealthy, background growing up. The whole relationship with him and his brother shows how people really are the same inside and there is equality because one of them made it so why didn't the other one? It's up to the individual choices, and Robby made bad choices.

TERESA: I would take this over Maya [Angelou] any day, even though it's harder to read, because like yeah, how you said, he presents himself as equal and not better than everybody and doesn't dwell on things like racism. Even though he talks about it, it didn't hold him back. This story gave me a feeling of like, equality and hope. Even though it was sad too.

Laura's opening comment, that she liked Wideman's narrator because he was "humble about his accomplishments," echoes her earlier comment "You can't have people saying 'I'm so different, I'm so special'" and, in its own way, is consistent with her desire to put "rednecks and kids who don't try in the basement and shut the door." For Laura, difference was a quality to hide, ignore, or obscure. According to the emotioned rules in place at Laurel Canyons, to do otherwise was to invite conflict and to participate, paradoxically, in promoting inequality. This emotioned rule was, of course, predicated in part on the logic of multiculturalism itself, which in its more benign forms insists that "we're all the same on the inside." But this rule clashed with other emotioned rules derived from more critically inflected versions of multiculturalism, like that promoted in Elizabeth's class, and the confusion plagued Laura and her classmates throughout the year.

In addition to emotioned rules that attempted to manage how students felt about difference, Elizabeth and I also attempted to teach students how to feel about feeling itself: when and which feelings were appropriate, where to express them, how to use them and for what purpose. Indeed, emotioned rules about feeling were a source of considerable confusion and conflict in Elizabeth's classroom, as Elizabeth attempted to engage students' curiosity and passion while also insisting that they critically (and dispassionately) analyze their own assumptions—often the very things they felt most passionately about.

Elizabeth worked hard to show her students the emotional pleasures that came from intellectual engagement, from reading and writing about complex topics. Passion, as Mike put it to me one day during class, was Elizabeth's "thing." For Elizabeth, thinking and questioning, exploring the complexities of an issue rather than rushing to resolve it neatly into a cliché or easy answer, held its own kinds of emotional pleasures: "I know it's crazy," she half-joked with her students, "but thinking about these questions can be fun! It's rewarding to try to understand a complicated issue or just not jump to easy conclusions or regurgitate what your parents taught you. Caring about this stuff is an important part of being an independent adult. You want me to treat you like adults. You have to think like adults, and stop letting your parents and your other teachers or your friends do your thinking for you."

But Elizabeth also privileged critical thinking and analysis, and as she herself acknowledged, passion and critical thinking didn't always go hand in hand. Much of the tension between these two rules surfaced in grading, a practice Elizabeth participated in because she had to (she was required to post students' grades on a regular basis so that parents and students would know where a student stood). She believed that grading could be useful at times, and her sense of truthfulness ensured that she was not a teacher who gave high grades easily. To be objective, Elizabeth based her grading standards on how carefully students analyzed texts, not necessarily on their engagement and passion, which was too subjective, though she stressed these characteristics heavily in class. The students zeroed in on the discrepancy. "She wants us to be all, like, we care about this and this is wrong and how we feel about it, but when it comes to the grading, it's my way or the highway, just like every other class. Did you put in enough quotes? Did you proofread? Did you give an analysis of the text? When, like, in class, it's about how we feel, not our analysis, you know?" Laura complained. Other students agreed. Elizabeth was a hard grader, and grades unfairly privileged analysis over passion. The confusion sometimes clouded Elizabeth's responses to students during class discussion as well. She often began discussion by eliciting students' affective responses and encouraging students to voice their engagement with the text. But when students expressed dislike, or when they expressed a response tinged with racism, Elizabeth switched tactics and exhorted students to think critically, be objective, and analyze the text rather than react emotionally to it.

In retrospect, I can see how attention to the contradictions embedded in the emotioned rules that structure our pedagogies, and to the conflicting emotioned performances these roles demand of students, would have helped Elizabeth and me understand students' responses, particularly to matters of race. Below, an extended scene from Elizabeth's classroom highlights these contradicting emotioned performances at work.

"You don't like to stand for the flag salute?" Laura asked me one morning in early January. She settled back into her seat, as the cheery voice of the student assistant who recited the pledge each morning faded from the loudspeaker mounted in a corner of the room.

"Why do you say that?" I asked.

"You never stand for the flag salute in the morning. This is like the first class I've ever had where the teachers—well, you're not our teacher, but Ms. Reed doesn't stand either most of the time."

Today Elizabeth was at the board, trying to pump some life into what had become a clear case of winter doldrums in the class. "What do these texts mean to *you* as a reader and a writer?" she wrote. She underlined "you" twice. Several students had slumped in their seats during the flag salute, but about half the class stood, as they did every day, with their hands over their hearts.

"I think I'm just patriotic in a different way, I guess," I said, responding to Laura.

Elizabeth had finished writing on the board and caught the conversation. "It's sort of like, you know, how different people have different ways of expressing their religious and spiritual beliefs?" she offered. "Like some read the Bible, and some go to church, and some do charity, and some go to temple, some spend time with nature . . ."

"I think you should do all of that," Laura said. "I try to read the Bible every day, and I always go to church, and sometimes there we do like charity work. That's the goal."

"Right," I said. "But other people express their beliefs differently, you know? Like some practice meditation, and some are Jewish, so they go to temple."

I remember feeling for a moment that the right lesson—plurality, difference, tolerance—had been offered and learned. But then Laura said, "Those people aren't saved though. Not if they haven't accepted Jesus."

When I listen to this moment now, on the tape, I recall the apprehension I felt and the corresponding hesitation that characterized Elizabeth's and my responses. We both understood that it was potentially dangerous to discuss religious beliefs with students. A few years ago, when Elizabeth had designed a unit in her Introduction to Humanities course around the theme of mortality—exploring how different cultures expressed ideas about the afterlife in art and literature—the unit immediately drew criticism from parents, who felt that mortality was too dark a theme for high-school-age students. "I wanted them to see that religion grows out of complexity and uncertainty. It doesn't or shouldn't be a way of shielding yourself from [them]. But parents were concerned that talking about death with kids would turn them into murderers, after Columbine," Elizabeth recalled. Eventually the unit was allowed into the curriculum, but Elizabeth remembered how stressful it had been, defending the unit to parents, making a formal presentation to the school board and fielding their questions. She was thus careful in her answers to Laura.

"That's what *you* believe," I said to Laura. By now, the whole class was listening. "But other people believe differently, and in a democratic country like ours, everyone has the right to whatever religious beliefs they choose, right?"

"The pastor in my church last week," Rich offered from a few desks away, "he was saying how that's true, about democracy, but like, he said like Afghanistan and the countries behind 9/11—it's not democracy they need. They need Christianity."

Earlier that year, Elizabeth had been with the students during the 9/11 terrorist attacks. I was not at Laurel Canyons that morning because of a faculty meeting in my department. Later, Elizabeth recounted her outrage that the school had refused to send students home. "These kids need to be with their families," she said again and again as we talked about that day. "But they just continued on as if nothing had happened." Indeed, in the days following September 11, "returning to normalcy" was the phrase the administration used as they encouraged teachers to refrain from talking about the terrorist attacks. (Discussions were to be left to the homeroom teacher, who was allowed one day to talk with students about how they were feeling.) After that, teachers were strongly encouraged to focus on regular lessons and "allow the students to return to normalcy." Although students talked about 9/11 informally throughout the year, it was never made part of the any class discussions beyond that first-period homeroom on the raw day after the attacks. As you'll see in the rest of the vignette, students' thoughts about terrorism and 9/11 were carefully couched in what they saw as appropriate school language, where dispassionate questioning and Socratic debate replace emotional engagement, which is reserved for multicultural texts that describe long-ago injustices.

"Okay," Elizabeth countered Rich, "but do you believe that everyone should be allowed to believe in whatever religion or even patriotism they choose?"

"In theory, yes," Rich said. "But that's what led to 9/11 and people killing people in the U.S. and hating us. I don't think it's really fair, like, they should not judge us just because of our economy. They should be all, everyone is the same inside. It's like we do that, but no one else does."

"Exactly," Laura agreed.

"Wait," I said. "Religious freedom led to 9/11? How?"

Elizabeth added, "But there's a difference between recognizing our common humanity or not judging people and telling people they have to believe in your religion."

"I think they weren't told about Christ, and so they weren't guided by him," Laura said.

"And that's why the terrorist attacks happened?" Elizabeth said.

"Well that's one reason."

"But in a democracy everyone has the right to believe as they wish and to express those beliefs in their own way," I said.

"Even if you express your beliefs by killing people?" Laura asked.

"Of course not," I replied. "Nobody thinks that you should kill people to express your beliefs. I mean within parameters, like that you don't infringe on other's rights. So everyone can choose different ways to express patriotism, and in fact we're free to feel unpatriotic if we choose."

"That's what we mean by tolerance," Elizabeth added.

"I don't see why you would be tolerant of murderers," Laura said.

"We're talking about being tolerant of religious difference, not murder."

"Is that like how we're tolerant of races, but not, like, racism?"

"I'm not sure I follow you."

"You know, how we're like, all races are equal and you can't judge, but when white people are racist, then you're not going to be tolerant of that. I don't think we're all like, 'Oh, that's just different, how they are in the South, and you can't judge them,' which I think is true because you can't really say how you'd be if you had their life. I don't know. I just don't think, in here, it's like we really want to be tolerant of *everything*, even 9/11, but like, you can't be tolerant of that."

Elizabeth glanced at me, eyebrows raised. The bell had already rung, signaling that class was beginning, and students were showing signs of restlessness with the discussion. Elizabeth asked students to get into their writing groups. I pulled a desk up to Laura's group. As we were waiting for everyone to get settled, Laura turned to me and continued the conversation:

"I still think that if more people like, cared about God, then 9/11 wouldn't have happened."

"So, you think that everyone should be Christian? And that would prevent terrorism?"

"Yeah. Because no Christian would have done that. They weren't guided by Jesus," Laura said.

"But Christians have killed people, sometimes even because they think they're 'guided by Jesus,'" I countered. "So how do you know that being Christian would prevent people from killing?"

"Christians wouldn't kill other Christians, so if everyone was Christian, then no one would get killed," Rich said.

"But Christians have killed other Christians," I said.

"Then they weren't real Christians," Laura answered.

The students' uncritical acceptance of the political and religious views of those bruised, post-9/11 months was as frustrating to me as their most offensive racist utterances. But Elizabeth and I, in our own responses to 9/11, were perhaps more easily blinded than we might otherwise have been to the emotioned rules at play in her classroom and the confusion these rules created not only for the students but also for us as we struggled toward coherent pedagogical responses to what sometimes seemed like extreme ideological difference. Throughout the discussion above, for example, the

students, Elizabeth, and I struggle with the contradictory emotioned va-
lences of the key concepts of critical pedagogy analyzed in the preceding
pages: difference and sameness, inclusion and exclusion, passionate engagement and critical analysis. On the one hand, the vignette makes clear that
all of us, in our own ways, have been schooled to fear difference: the flutter
of apprehension and corresponding hesitation that mark Elizabeth's and
my responses to the students' patriotic and religious utterances, the students' 9/11-inspired equation of difference with terrorism, their belief that
terrorism can be prevented by the elimination of difference. Throughout
the discussion, fear of difference is managed by multiculturally inflected
attempts to assert sameness. (Even Elizabeth and I manage our reaction to
the students' views by reminding ourselves that we were once like them.)
There is a related confusion about inclusion and exclusion that structures
the vignette, as Laura draws moral lines about terrorism and then attempts
to give this line-drawing legitimacy and currency via the rhetorics of multiculturalism that Elizabeth and I invoke. "It's like how all races are equal
and you can't judge, but when white people are racist, then you're not going
to be tolerant of that."

And of course, there are the contradictory emotioned rules about passion
and engagement, on the one hand, and critical thinking and analysis, on the
other. Students were often exhorted to feel passionately about intellectual
endeavors. They were encouraged to feel outrage over injustices and to emotionally engage in the reading and writing they were assigned. But displays
of passion that didn't follow guidelines in terms of when and where they
were expressed were often quickly censored, and critical analysis, which was
understood as emotionally neutral, was instead privileged. Indeed, looking back through the materials I collected at Laurel Canyons, I can see not
only how Elizabeth and I invoked the need for critical analysis at moments
when we felt most threatened by, or helpless to counter, extreme expressions of racism or other forms of intolerance but also how we used fear to
steer students away from those expressions. "When you get to college," I
told students, "you're going to need to know how to do this stuff [critical
analysis and close reading]," a point both Elizabeth and Julie, the inclusion
teacher, often echoed. "People in the real world aren't going to care how
you feel; they're going to care about whether you can write clearly."

In the 9/11 discussion above, students were encouraged to engage *texts*
with passion ("What does this text mean to *you*?" Elizabeth wrote on the
board) but were subtly discouraged from expressing their passions about
religion or patriotism. Both Elizabeth and I steered students toward a more
dispassionate Socratic questioning about religion and patriotism, two topics
that Elizabeth knew from experience could get her in hot water at Laurel

Canyons. Both of us avoided direct or emotional statements of our own positions, even though, in our private conversations, we expressed vehement opposition to the reigning patriotic sentiments of those first post-9/11 months, when, as Elizabeth put it, you couldn't walk two feet without stumbling over somebody's flag and their desire for vengeance.

Despite her professed hatred of poetry, Laura got her first "Highly Satisfactory" grade on her essay on poetry. She based her essay on a pivotal discussion she and Elizabeth had about assumptions. She learned, from this conversation, that assumptions shaped judgment and perception, and that critical thinking required awareness of this process. In her essay, she moved between this new understanding and her old belief that Elizabeth made things too complex. "Trying to look into the deep side of everything is a waste of time," she maintained, but she was nonetheless pleased with her final essay on poetry. In her essay, she acknowledged that her initial response to poetry had been based largely on misunderstanding and that she now understood that poetry was about "questioning your assumptions." She began her essay with a quote from Adrienne Rich's "When We Dead Awaken: Writing as Re-Vision": "Until we know and understand the assumptions in which we are drenched we cannot know ourselves." In the rest of the essay, she argued that Emanuel's goal in her poem "Frying Trout While Drunk" was not actually to "just write about a bunch of white trash alcoholics" but to reveal to the reader that it is wrong to assume that those who drink are weak or to try to categorize people as good or bad: "I think the whole message of the poem is that there is no black and white, no simple answer. These are assumptions of society. We live in a culture where there is a right or wrong for everything, and things are either good or bad. Lynn is trying to make us overcome these ideas, because her mother has good and bad qualities. So the readers don't know how to perceive the mother, which was exactly Lynn's point. Is she good or bad? Lynn says it doesn't matter; she can be both."

The sense of not-quite-realized potential in Laura's essay reminds me of a moment described earlier in this book, when Mike was watching *The Color Purple* and commented softly, as the lights came up, that "white people suck." He made this comment at the end of class, as students were packing up and heading for the door, and I didn't get a chance to ask him about it until later.

"You know, the other day, when we were watching the movie and you said white people sucked?"

"I didn't say that," Mike said quickly.

"You didn't?"

"No."

"Come on. I heard you say it. I was sitting right here."

"Why would I say that? That's totally stupid. I mean, I'm white. Why would I say white people suck? Like, maybe the guy in that movie sucked but I would never say that about white people."

"Why not?"

"Because, dude, you don't criticize your own race. That's like, obvious, from this movie and everything else we read. You don't see Black people like, criticizing themselves for like, whatever rap or ghetto lifestyle. So you don't see white people criticize themselves either. Even if they deserve it. See, each race criticizes the other. That's how it works. Even in here, we're all, 'everyone's equal,' but, I think, it's still just like, each race against each other."

"What do you mean?"

"Well, it's like, think about it. It's a segregated school, it's all white people here, and we watch segregated movies and books, about how like, Black people this, white people that. But we're supposed to like, be less racist. It doesn't make sense. They should show *Die Hard*, if they want to like, end racism. Where people don't care about race, and it makes you think. That's my question. Why do we watch this shit? She [Elizabeth] wants us to question, so I'm like, that's my question. But it's probably not what she had in mind."

Actually, Elizabeth would have loved Mike's question, had he ever voiced it in class. His response makes clear the difficulties of the situated readings of students that Elizabeth and I, as teacher and researcher, performed throughout the year. It is difficult to describe Mike's stance toward race or to know with any certainty what he has learned about race from his participation in Elizabeth's class. Any attempt to do so will be at best partial, a "moral fiction," as Hicks (2002) might phrase it, reflecting certain ways of theorizing, highlighting some problems, downplaying others.

Most multicultural and antiracist education has been oriented away from the ethereal and incremental change that characterizes Mike's and Laura's work in Elizabeth's class. Our pedagogies, as Elizabeth Ellsworth (1997) reminds us, are not designed to help us understand the chimeras of potential in Mike's response or in Laura's essay. Antiracist pedagogy tends to be predicated on an illusion of control that the fleeting potential-filled moments like those above do not sustain. Ellsworth calls on us to replace that illusion with the recognition that teaching is a messier and more inconclusive affair than most of our educational theories and practices make it out to be. To replace the illusion of control, Ellsworth investigates ways of teaching that are predicated on "the impossibility of teaching" (55), including "the inchoate realm of emotion" (57). But what I hope the last two chapters have shown is that while the realm of emotion may be inchoate and thus teaching in some sense, as Ellsworth maintains, is impossible, emotion is also structured by school and by our own practices. Consequently, persuading students *is* possible but not, perhaps, via the teaching traditions we currently employ, a point Ellsworth also makes in her emphasis on the possibilities of pedagogies structured around psychoanalysis, film, and magic realism, all of which tap "the inchoate realm of emotion" in ways traditional schooling does not.

What Ellsworth describes as the overly managed, rational approach to education I have come to think of in terms of time, and rhetoric. We approach learning in terms of chronos, rather than kairos. *Kairos* refers to the ways a given moment and context for communication both calls for and constrains one's speech. It refers to the exigencies and constraints of time, place, culture, and audience that together create particular discursive situations. Whereas *chronos* refers to chronological or sequential time, *kairos* signals a time in between, a moment of undetermined length that holds discursive promise and opportunity. Chronos is quantitative; kairos, qualitative. Chronos exists in the realm of reason and rationality; kairos in the realm of the affective and unconscious.

Chronos-oriented approaches, including multiculturalism, critical pedagogies, and pedagogies that interrogate whiteness and privilege, are dependent on readings of students that are situated in the insider-outsider mapping of critical discourse: they assume an ideological or political problem in students that we, as experts, as antiracists (insiders), must remedy. They are rooted in a conception of teaching that not only assumes rationality and reason are the keys to persuasion but also views emotions negatively, as problems to be worked through or overcome—student hostility, defensiveness, anger, or shame. Chronos-oriented classroom approaches work independently from institutions and institutional rhetoric and rely exclusively on classroom activities and curricula to achieve their goals. When practitioners of such approaches take institutional factors into account, they tend to view institutions as barriers to student change rather than seeing the institutional and cultural life of a school as a resource for persuasive action. And chronos-oriented approaches proceed linearly across time, beginning with the deficit of racism and culminating in a final product—the antiracist student.

Two years after I completed my research at Laurel Canyons, I interviewed Elizabeth again. As she reflected on her goals as a teacher and the challenges she faced that year, Elizabeth intuited an alternative to chronos-oriented approaches to teaching. She talked about how matters of race are rooted in people's affective lives and how emotions are mediated by context. She talked about needing room, as a teacher, to work nonlinearly across time, moving backward and forward as necessary in ongoing and mutual efforts toward change. She talked about process over product. "These are people-in-process, the students. I don't think you can pin them down at 'point A'—racist, ignorant, whatever—and then somehow take them through a series of hoops that leads them to Point B and call it a day."

What would a kairotic, emotionally responsive antiracist pedagogy look like? How might we begin to unpack our own discursive investments in particular emotioned stances and rules? As Gorzelsky writes, we must "use our scholarship to examine our own rhetorical habits, both in scholarly writing and in our day-to-day interactions, particularly pedagogical interactions" (2005, 29) like the ones I've described here. Such scrutiny, Gorzelsky writes, leads inexorably to experimentation, classroom risk taking, and change. In the next chapter, I narrate the last months of the school year I spent at Laurel Canyons, and, following Gorzelsky, I scrutinize our scholarly writing—particularly our metaphors for whiteness—with the goal of moving us toward more persuasive rhetorics of change.

5

BEYOND WHITE PRIVILEGE
JUNE AT LAUREL CANYONS

In *Literacy and Racial Justice: The Politics of Learning after* Brown v. Board of Education, Catherine Prendergast (2003) extends one of the most generative and pervasive metaphors for whiteness—that of whiteness as property—to the arena of literacy. Prendergast argues that throughout American history literacy education has been "managed and controlled in myriad ways to rationalize and ensure white domination" and that whites have been "willing to commit crimes large and small in order to maintain their exclusive franchise on . . . literacy institutions" (5). Indeed, she argues, whites have an "investment in literacy" and hence one of the key components of the ideology of literacy—the collective beliefs about its definition, purpose, and utility—has been the notion that literacy and its institutions, including schools and universities, belong to whites. Prendergast's analysis, particularly the economic language she uses to describe the relationship between whiteness and literacy (whites have a "franchise on" and "investment in" literacy and its institutions), derives from critical race theory and its lexicon of economic metaphors for whiteness, which is likened to a wage, property, or investment (see, for example, David Roediger's *The Wages of Whiteness: Race and the Making of the American Working Class*, George Lipsitz's *The Possessive Investment in Whiteness: How White People Profit from Identity Politics*, and Cheryl Harris's "Whiteness as Property"). Harris explains the power of the metaphor succinctly: "whiteness . . . meets the functional criteria of property. Specifically, the law has accorded 'holders' of whiteness the same privileges and benefits accorded holders of other types of property" (1731).

One of the privileges of whiteness, of course, is education. As Gloria Ladson-Billings and William Tate (1995) note, if whiteness is property, then we need to consider the role of whiteness in education, as "property relates to education in explicit and implicit ways." Those with "'better property,'" Ladson-Billings and Tate write, "are entitled to 'better' schools'" (53–54). Thus school inequality may be a literal matter of property-tax funding, but it is also a matter of race privilege and the power of whiteness to "entitle" one to "better" schools. Recent ethnographies of schooling document the racial dimensions of the competitive struggle to ensure continued white ownership of schooling. For example, in *Doing School: How We Are Creating a Generation of Stressed Out, Materialistic, and Miseducated Students* (2001), Denise Clark Pope describes a high school in an affluent California suburb, a place where nearly all of the students graduate and attend prestigious universities. It is a place, in Pope's words, where people are "obsessed" with being the best and with helping their children acquire top credentials. "The drive to succeed," she writes, "has led some parents to employ expensive agencies to tutor their children to get high scores on the SATs. . . . Other families turn to web sites that sell high-priced college application essays guaranteed to get students into ivy league schools" (166–167). At a gathering of local third-graders, Pope notes that the children speak in earnest of their hopes to attend Stanford or Harvard when they grow up. "I want to be rich and drive a Lexus," one youngster remarks. "So I need to get A's in school" (167). Pope describes the effects on these students' intellectual and moral development, as well as physical and mental health, of their struggle to cash in on their ownership of education. Although not all of the focal students in Pope's study are white, and although Pope attempts to bracket race out of her discussion (it is "beyond the scope" of her study, she writes in a footnote), the racial dimensions of "doing school" are apparent to the students of color she talks to. About one of her Latina focal students, for example, Pope writes that

> Teresa perceives a difference in the way the white and Mexican students are treated at school. She associates qualities such as whiteness, wealth, and power (at least power over the school curriculum) with the students who live in the suburbs. She sees some sort of connection between the amount of taxes one pays and an ability to influence school decisions such as who teaches and what material is taught in school programs. She is convinced that the honors program and other programs where "white" students are well represented are "better" because "white parents" want to ensure that their kids get into college and will "make sure" the program is "good." (78)

Teresa's perceptions about the connections among race, privilege, and schooling suggest that white ownership of education, particularly literacy, as Prendergast makes clear, is embedded in layers of school practices (honors programs, curricular choices, school funding) and in concomitant decisions about who is included in particular programs and who is not. They also suggest that the manipulation and cheating that Pope documents are raced activities, that "doing school"—what she defines as manipulating school to maximize one's own advantage—perpetuates racism and racial domination.

In *Dividing Classes: How the Middle Class Negotiates and Rationalizes School Advantage*, Ellen Brantlinger (2003) describes the phenomenon Teresa intuits. Brantlinger shows how "white members of the professional class" work to "secure the best of what schools have to offer for [their] own children" (xi). In her study, Brantlinger describes white parents who exert considerable influence on school practices by pressuring school personnel to put their preferences into effect (58). For these parents, "children's school success is part of a status competition among parents," and they thus preferred, and worked to maintain, segregated and stratified schools that benefited middle-class students. Both of these studies, Brantlinger's in particular, remind us that literacy is yet another invisible advantage in the "knapsack" of white privilege, to borrow Peggy McIntosh's (1992) phrase, a commodity that whites can cash in on by simple virtue of being white.

But consider for a moment that most students in the United States do not, upon graduation from high school, attend elite, selective-admissions four-year institutions. Consider what John Alberti (2001) calls a major class division in American higher education: the gap between first-tier selective admissions schools and second-tier open-registration, regional two- and four-year colleges—what he calls "working class" colleges (565). These schools, not elite, competitive universities, comprise the majority of institutions of higher education in the U.S. Many of them are distinctly vocational in orientation. And consider that, even including these schools, only approximately 30 percent of white people in the U.S. between the ages of twenty-five and twenty-nine have a bachelor's degree at all.

Alberti helps me think about the postgraduation aspirations of Laurel Canyons students and their relationship to race. Listening to students talk about life after high school in turn helps me think differently about the assumptions I have made in my own teaching, as well as in the original conceptualization of this research, about whiteness, privilege, and racism. Here is Laura, talking about her postgraduation plans:

> I'll probably go to State [a local college with a noncompetitive admissions policy]. I got into Northwestern, though, and I really thought I might go there. My parents have saved for a long time for me to go to college, and they are real encouraging. They went to college, and like, they know it was important. But I know if I go somewhere expensive, it will be harder for them to pay for my brother, and they have to think about his college, in two years, you know? I don't want to put that kind of burden on them.

But my dad, he's like, Laura, it's your decision. We support you. But you
know, it's ridiculous to spend that kind of money when you don't have
to. It's like, you can get the same education at a place like State. And
honestly, it will be nicer for my mom, if I stay around here, even live at
home. We're real close, and it would be hard for her, to be so far away.

Other students have similarly modest postsecondary plans: technical
school, junior college, beauty school. I ask Chris what he plans to do. His
father and brother both have bachelor's degrees from research universities
in the state.

"What are your plans for next year?" I ask. "Are you applying for college?"

"No," he says, drawing out the word in an embarrassed shrug. "I don't
think so. I'm not, like, 'college material' or whatever, you know? I'm not
good at school. I just want to get a job, and you can get good jobs without
going to college. I might go to Western Valley [a local two-year technical
school], and they'll teach you, like, about cars or computers. My cousin did
that, and he makes a lot of money now and has his own apartment."

And yet, Laurel Canyons is moderately high achieving, with slightly
higher than average scores on state standardized tests. The median home
values in the district are above the state average, and fewer than 6 percent of
the students qualify as "low-income." The school serves an overwhelmingly
white student population, most of whom come from middle-class homes.
The population of adults in the district who have college degrees is over 30
percent (above the national and state percentages), and the property values are above state averages. Still, most of Laurel Canyons' students have
no college plans. Indeed, the overall percentage of the state's population
who had a bachelor's degree was 16 percent at the time of this research,
a fact I had to repeat several times as I talked to colleagues about this research. In this way, Laurel Canyons students only tentatively possess, or
in some cases choose to forego, one of the fundamental material privileges
associated with whiteness: higher education. In this final chapter, I want
to problematize assumptions about white students in yet another way, by
complicating the economic metaphors of white privilege in general and of
white "ownership" of education and literacy in particular. I'll argue here
for a view of whiteness as a dynamic, emotioned, rhetorical process rather
than "property"—metaphoric or actual—that gives way to racism as a
rational way to hang on to what one owns. Laurel Canyons students do
not support the widely held belief that middle-class white students have
straightforward access to higher education and the economic and cultural
privileges that it confers. This belief derives from a familiar dichotomy
that pits privilege, literacy, enfranchisement, and whiteness on one side
against nonwhite, working-class disenfranchisement and illiteracy on the

other. Laurel Canyons students exist in socioeconomic borderlands beyond these categories. In this last chapter, I draw from the last few months of the study, as students made postgraduation plans. I focus on Michelle's experiences with a high-stakes literacy requirement and on her plans for the future, and I examine the "wages" her whiteness supposedly confers on her in terms of literacy and access to higher education. In doing so, I hope to move beyond the dichotomies named above. This up-close view allows the dynamic and shifting relationships among literacy, access, and race to come into focus, suggesting that literacy, though it may be white property, as Prendergast suggests, is contested property, with a market value that is difficult to pin down. Ownership of it is a dynamic, emotioned process that involves rhetorical, curricular, and institutional struggle. Recognizing that privilege, access, even literacy itself, are emotioned processes rather than static properties owned by whites leads to a rethinking of pedagogies of whiteness. Disentangling the associations between race and access will help antiracist educators recognize and address some of the limitations of classroom interrogations of whiteness. The failures of pedagogies of whiteness may stem in part from the ways economic metaphors for whiteness (including the widely used metaphor of the "knapsack" of white privileges, a point I'll return to) do not adequately capture the struggles for ownership of literacy—and the unsteady, emotioned value of both racial identity and literacy—as they play out in school and in students' lived experiences.

I have argued throughout the previous chapters that racist discourses at Laurel Canyons were rarely motivated by students' experiences of race privilege or desire to secure or maintain race privilege. Embedded in this argument is a central point about "privilege": it is a process rather than a property, a point derived not just from my work at Laurel Canyons but also from recent work by whiteness researchers. In her recent study of race at three elementary schools, for example, Amanda Lewis (2004) focuses on the schools' role in ascribing racial identity to students. She argues that efforts to understand how racial identities influence educational outcomes often overlook the ways schools create racial meanings and promote particular racial identities. Schools, Lewis argues, teach the rules of racial classification and provide a space where students can practice them, and hence they are "race-making" institutions. Schools are not only places where white privilege produces unequal outcomes (as implied by the whiteness-as-property metaphor); they are places where individuals and groups create, learn, and negotiate racial meanings, places where the property of whiteness fluctuates in value, depending on institutional and social contexts. Pamela Perry's (2002) study of two high schools makes a similar claim and suggests that rules of racial classification are intensely local, involving wide variation within broad racial descriptors: there are different ways of being white in different local contexts, and the meaning and value of whiteness shifts across these contexts, making terms like *privilege* difficult to pin down. At heart in both of these studies is a desire to understand how white students develop their racial subjectivities in school and a sense that such understanding is central to future possibilities for racial equity in the United States. If, as Lewis and Perry argue, schools play a role in the production of race as a social category both through implicit and explicit lessons and through school practices, then struggles over literacy, as I show in this chapter, are part of the apparatus of that production, part of a process by which racial ascriptions are made and racial meanings and values assigned.

Although, as I am suggesting, our metaphors for white privilege need to be more complex, I do not want to lose sight of the fundamental realities of racial inequality and race privilege in and out of school. In the stories I tell in this final chapter, for example, and in the emphasis I place on the shifting and contradictory nature of white privilege, racism was nonetheless at work at Laurel Canyons in the choices available to the students and parents and in the educational and social power they were able to purchase for themselves (albeit at sometimes serious cost). This is power that, as several studies have amply documented, is not accessible—or not accessible to the same degree—to students of color and their families. The system of whiteness in place in public education and elsewhere is very real. But the *metaphor* of whiteness as property and the conception of racism as a response to the need to protect that property do not adequately capture the complexity of that system. We need to interrogate the metaphor of privilege as property, a metaphor that sometimes obscures the ways in which privilege is purchased, negotiated, sometimes rejected, and most important, emotionally experienced.

Lewis (2004) notes, most white students in the United States attend all-white schools; most live in highly racially segregated neighborhoods and have little regular, substantial contact with people of other races (12). In this sense, the demographics of Laurel Canyons—its overwhelming whiteness—are not particularly unusual. And yet this stark racial segregation tends to obscure other kinds of diversity; a closer look at Laurel Canyons reveals contradictory demographic details. One student's mother lacked a college degree and worked as a beautician, but his father had a degree from a university and worked in management; another student's father worked construction, but her mother was a school teacher. Mike lived in a big house in one of the wealthier subdivisions but worked two jobs, at a drive-through window and at a clothing store in the mall. Laura had the resources to go to college but chose to stay close to home, partly for financial reasons. The school itself reflected this socioeconomic ambiguity. The school's Web site boasts that 77 percent of its graduating seniors seek postsecondary education and 72 percent take the SAT, but for most students, postsecondary meant junior college, local business administration or technical colleges, or local state schools. Few students at Laurel Canyon went on to study at a competitive-admissions university, and only a handful went on to local four-year schools. Eighteen percent of the students were, at the time of the study, enrolled in special education programs, and the high school's state standardized test pass rate was just below 70 percent. Only 6 percent of the school's students took the advanced-placement test.

When I asked students at Laurel Canyons to talk about why they chose their postgraduation plans, they spoke of the difficulty of amassing simultaneously different kinds of capital: economic, sociocultural, academic. Some students had the grades and the money to go to college, but they chose a technical school because they didn't want to saddle a working parent with sole care for a younger sibling. Some had parents who could afford to pay for college but didn't have the grades, couldn't complete the graduation requirements, or felt that college would take them too far from home; others lacked the financial resources but had taken advanced-placement classes and had straight A's and the solid encouragement of their teachers. Some couldn't imagine leaving behind friends. Others had parents, themselves with university degrees, who didn't believe college was worth the money and felt that their own college degrees hadn't proved to be worth much. The students' experiences demonstrate the difficulty of defining whiteness in terms of class privilege or disenfranchisement and highlight the complexity of access to education, which emerges in the students' experiences not as something owned by whites but rather as a shifting site of varying value and availability.

Michelle was a case in point. She was one of a number of students who had difficulty passing the research paper portion of the senior project, a requirement for graduation. Although the senior project was progressive in its intentions and design—it allowed for multiple literacy skills, asked students to participate meaningfully in a community project of their choice, and was widely viewed as a more authentic and student-centered assessment than the timed writing exams other districts used—the research paper portion of it was actually quite traditional. It asked students to develop a thesis, state it formally in the introduction, support it with library research, and document sources by using Modern Language Association (MLA) format.

In Michelle's eyes, the senior project was an unnecessary gatekeeper, the school's way of boosting its reputation at the expense of its students' needs: "The whole senior project thing? And like how you have to write a research paper? They're just trying to keep up with Lincoln [a neighboring school] and be like, our kids are so smart, and our scores are so high," she told me during class one day. Several parents, including Michelle's, echoed this view and believed the school had gone overboard with the requirement, which was seen as too difficult for high school students, many of whom would not attend college and would therefore, presumably, have no need for such research skills. As Elizabeth perceived it, parents wielded considerable power in the school, and their complaints about the senior project made it harder for her to do her job. She often talked about parents who "greased the wheels" for their children in ways that undermined the education she was trying to provide—parents who manipulated teachers into passing students who didn't meet requirements or sought a learning-disabilities diagnosis for their children to secure extra time and more lenient standards for projects. "You have to be careful," she said often, "because if you get one complaint [from a parent], one parent phone call can change school policy." And for Elizabeth, a parent complaint could lead to administrative and school board review of her teaching, which in turn could mean even less freedom in the classroom than she already had. Brantlinger (2003) describes this phenomenon as a "parentocracy," a term that refers to the control white and middle-class parents have over schools and teachers. As she writes, parentocracies emerge when middle-class parents believe that advocating for school advantage for their children is integral to being a good parent. These parents often "unite in collective action to secure advantages for children of their class" (Brantlinger, 11). Typically, the members of a parentocracy work to ensure that their children are placed in the highest tracks with the "best" teachers. But at Laurel Canyons, parents also worked to have learning disabilities diagnosed in their children, because the label came with extra time on tests and ensured that less rigorous standards would be used in evaluating the student's work, thus making it easier for the student to graduate. And, as we'll see below, parents sometimes advocated for a curriculum that was less rigorous, or "elitist," in parents' words, often out of fear that high standards would work against their child's success.

When Michelle and several other students received no credit on the rough drafts of their research papers for failing to document library sources properly, parents began to advocate against the senior project, arguing that it was discriminatory. In a long letter one of the parents sent to Elizabeth and to the school administration, the parent protested the senior project and its literacy requirements as a gatekeeper to middle-class prosperity. At the same time, this parent expressed resistance to the particular kind of white middle-class-ness the school implicitly promoted via its literacy requirements: "Graduation should be about fun memories and walking across the stage with friends," the parent wrote, "not worrying about whether you wrote a paper with proper footnotes. . . . Not all students are meant to be a mathematician or journalist or doctor. What about the average child?" She went on to discuss her sense that the school's curriculum discriminated against "average" students and argued that the literacy requirements most students would need in the workplace did not include knowledge of MLA citation conventions or library research skills.

Many parents at Laurel Canyons appeared to share this view, and thus they approached the senior project in ways that undermined its intent—helping students get around various aspects of its requirements, in some cases even helping students forge aspects of it. Laurel Canyons is in a state that has made the senior project a high-stakes graduation requirement. Nationwide, as the *Wall Street Journal* recently reported, many parents resent the time burdens senior projects place on their families and are convinced that the projects turn teachers into "nit-picking, power-wielding maniacs," determining students' futures by counting page numbers, combing through MLA citations looking for errors, or failing students' oral presentations on the smallest of details.

But parents, one administrator told me, "just don't understand what the school is trying to do." In his view,

At Lincoln and North High, they have super high SATs. But we've got kids who do everything right and then don't even apply. You tell them to take AP [advanced-placement] classes, take the SAT, apply to college, and their parents are like, college is too expensive, they're going to [the local junior college], and these are well-off parents! The same parents who complain the second anything goes wrong around here. The rural families would kill for those opportunities, and we can't get our high-achieving kids to have high aspirations. We have a five-year plan to raise aspirations, to start younger with the kids, get them psyched for college. It's straightforward with the rural community: you make sure they know the options, have access to financial aid, make sure their kids take the right classes, and we've done that here. We have open tracks, kids self-select, and you can see kids right off the farm in AP history and AP English and doing well. But you take these Crimson kids [kids from the well-off suburbs and townships that feed into the school], and they have everything, and they do well, and their parents are super involved in the school, and you get to the moment of college choice, and they'll take [the state school] or [community college], anything to save a buck, keep their kids close to them. They have this idea that it's all just foolish and a waste of time. It's like one of them said, my kid doesn't need a fancy diploma from a fancy school. Just make sure he graduates, and I'll take care of the rest. Mediocrity is our problem. A lot of parents can't imagine sending their kids off to college, can't afford it, maybe, but just don't want to imagine it.

The contradictory reversals at work here—where working-class whites take advantage of progressive school policies to send their children to college, while more privileged middle-class whites refuse to do so and instead use parentocratic tools to ensure "mediocrity" for their children—make clear that the notion of white ownership of literacy does not fully capture the complex relationship between privilege and schooling at Laurel Canyons. Literacy may be white property, as Prendergast has persuasively argued, but struggles over who owns it—manifest in conflicts over the senior project and in students' postgraduation plans—suggest that as much as whites may ratchet up the value of literacy to keep their own status and mark racial boundaries, they also exert a downward pressure on it, as they work to keep literacy affordable for themselves. As the value of literacy goes up, as literacy becomes more and more high-priced, whites at Laurel Canyons struggled against this inflation to ensure their share. Prendergast compellingly documents how racialized struggles over ownership of literacy take place in research projects, courtrooms, and other public venues. But as Michelle's experiences suggest, these struggles also play out in very personal, emotioned ways in the local context of the classroom.

Beyond the Invisible Knapsack of White Privilege

Indeed, the classroom is a site where the complexity of the relationship between whiteness and privilege is most obscured and where the need for exploration of that complexity is most severe. The growing body of scholarship on "critical pedagogies of whiteness" (Applebaum 2003) points to the myriad ways such pedagogies fall short. Kathy Hytten and John Warren (2003), Audrey Thompson (2003), and Lewis, Ketter, and Fabos (2001), for example, all write of white students who refuse to discuss racial injustice. Alice McIntyre (1997) describes how difficult it is for even well-intentioned white teachers to engage in critiques of white privilege. Much of this research, as I argued early on in this book, posits a characterization of white students as privileged—benefiting from an unjust racial hierarchy in the United States—and therefore as unwilling to engage with texts or ideas that critique privilege and suggest the need for social change, and much of it draws from one of the most powerful iterations of the whiteness-as-property metaphors, Peggy McIntosh's (1991) seminal "White Privilege: Unpacking the Knapsack." In this essay, McIntosh illustrates white privilege by describing a "knapsack," an "invisible package of unearned assets that [whites] can count on cashing in each day, but about which [whites are] meant to remain oblivious" (291). This formulation suggests that privilege is a tangible commodity one owns and can use like currency, trading it for other tangible commodities. Applebaum's discussion of her experiences teaching McIntosh's essay suggest the difficulty white students have in understanding how white privilege, conceptualized in this way, works:

> A number of months ago, after what I considered to be a good discussion of Peggy McIntosh's influential article, I asked my students to identify three examples of how privilege, in the sense that McIntosh articulates, works on our own campus. Among the responses I received to my requests for dominant group privileges that can be seen today on our campus, however, were:
>
>> Females get free drinks at the bars while
>>   males have to pay all the time.
>> Females get taken out on dates and the men pay for them.
>> Students who work in the dining hall get free food.
>> Being part of this university will get your foot
>>   in the door when you apply for a job.
>> Tall people have privilege in college basketball.
>> Blacks and other minorities have privilege because they get
>>   athletic scholarships and affirmative action benefits. (8)

Analyzing these responses, Applebaum points out the resistance embedded in her white students' seemingly willful misunderstanding of the concept of dominant group privilege: "Not only do some of my students fail to appreciate the systemic nature of dominant group privilege . . . they also do not see how the oppression of people of color systemically sustains and makes possible dominant group privilege" (8).

I have a slightly different interpretation of Applebaum's students' responses: her students do not appreciate the systemic nature of privilege because they don't experience privilege systemically. What they experience are "contradictions in subjective experiences and in educational discourses" (Levine-Rasky 2000, 274) of the sort I have chronicled at Laurel Canyons. What they experience is a system of privileges that is in flux and whose value is not guaranteed. In this way, to characterize whiteness as a wage that confers systemic privileges, that indicates a particular economic relationship to literacy, to see whiteness as a wage that can purchase literacy and whites as thus owning it is to miss much about the contested nature of literacy, race, and class.

Michelle had planned to attend a local community college with her best friend, Lisa, but that spring, her enthusiasm for this plan dimmed considerably. Lisa had decided to go to a four-year college, several miles to the south, because her parents believed she should do something with her life and get away from the "trashy elements" at the junior college. "You know, it's just a lot of the same kids from here and from Carville [a nearby working-class township], and it's very low-life," Lisa said in class one day, with a typical lack of tact.

Michelle snorted. "She means me." She turned to me, "Her mom thinks like I'm a bad influence. . . . That's why they won't let her go to [the junior college]. They want her to get away from me."

"It's kind of true," Lisa conceded. "They think if I go there I'll just hang out with the same high school crowd and it will bring me down."

I want to return for a moment to Michelle's beginning story, which stood out because of its focus on school:

I had this friend in junior high. I didn't go here. We lived in Centerpoint, where my mom is from, then, and I went to junior high there, and we moved because it's kind of a rough school, you know? Not as good as here. But in seventh grade, me and this girl, Sheila, were best friends, and she was Black. It didn't mean anything to me. We had like all our classes together, and if it was alphabetical we sat by each other because her name was right after mine. I didn't have a lot of friends there, because there are so many losers who live in that district, which is why we moved. But Sheila was cool. And we hung out all the time. She was really funny and would always crack me up. And we got in trouble in class a lot, we would like goof around, mouth off to teachers, and they were always like calling my parents and stuff. And one day, we got in trouble . . . and the teacher sent us to different rooms so we would stop talking and goofing around, and to me she was like, why do you hang out with her? She's getting you in trouble. She was all, Michelle, you're college material, you're going somewhere, and she's not, and she's bringing you down. I can see it happening. And I was all, whatever. It still pisses me off. I guess she thought, like because my dad has money, and like went to college, that I was all "college material," but you know what? I'm totally not. And my parents, they're fine with it. My sister went, but I'm all, I don't want to leave my friends, and my grades suck, and I'm just totally not college material. And my dad's like, that's fine. I think he doesn't want me to leave my mom, because then he'd have to deal with her. And my mom thinks college is expensive for what it is, you know? You can get the same thing at [the local community college], or even better, they have really good teachers there, and it costs like half the price for tuition. My mom just wants me to learn something useful so I can get a job, and she's always all, Michelle, what are they teaching you at that school? It's ridiculous, half the stuff we read in here, it's not going to help in the workforce, and my mom knows it. I think college is kind of overrated, if you ask me.

In fundamental respects, this is a story of white privilege and the education that whiteness can purchase. Michelle's whiteness garners a favorable impression of her from her teacher, which results in the kinds of encouragement that students need if they are going to succeed. And Michelle's parents, at least in part because they are white, possessed the resources to move out of a school district that was too "rough," thus ensuring a "better" education for their daughter. These are the kinds of privileges that are generally invisible to most whites, as McIntosh illustrates.

But at the same time, the issues Michelle's story raises—racism, educational access, the uses and usefulness of literacy, privilege—complicate the economic metaphors of whiteness as a "wage," "investment," "property," or "perk" one can pull out of a knapsack. Privilege in Michelle's narrative is not a static quantity that, as a white person, she owns and uses. Rather it emerges as a complex process that mutates and shifts across contexts. For Michelle, the "privilege" of literacy and access that her whiteness gives her is a commodity of unstable value, and she grasps it fleetingly. Positioned as possessing access to education—"you're college material," her teacher tells her—she is also alienated from it by her friendship with a person of color and, perhaps more complexly, by her own sense that education is more limiting than advantageous, an expensive waste that will take her away from friends and family and provide her with skills she and her family believe she won't need. None of this is to say that Michelle's access to literacy is less direct or less straightforward than, for example, her friend Sheila's or to suggest that racism—in this case both the teacher's personal racist assumptions and the more difficult-to-pin-down economic and institutional racism that permeates Michelle's family's decision to move and their ability to do so—doesn't have invidious consequences for both girls. But it is to say that if we want to help students understand systemic racial inequality, then we must begin to investigate with them the specific and complex ways in which whites "own" literacy and other privileges and to examine the dynamic, processual, and emotioned nature of that ownership.

Complicating this will be the difficulty of pinning down in any meaningful way the value and significance of what it means to be white at all. To say that Michelle is white without also signifying her socioeconomic class identity makes the racial designation almost meaningless. (Consider the connotative difference between "working-class white" and "middle-class white" in terms of what we assume about racial privilege and participation in systems of inequality). To say that she is white without a clear understanding of the relationship between whiteness and racism or of the relationship between racism and the emotioned positions students are persuaded, via their education, to adopt is also almost meaningless. But assigning a class identity to Michelle is difficult. Michelle and her family really can't be adequately described as either middle- or working-class, as part of a powerful and affluent parentocracy advocating for advantage for themselves via schooling, or as disempowered members of the working class, with all the educational inequality, discrimination, and alienation that such working-class status has usually entailed.

In the end, only a handful of the students I got to know in the course of my research at Laurel Canyons ended up going to four-year universities. Laura was one of them. She planned to go a local state school in the fall. She had decided to live at home though, to save money, and because, as she said, her own home was "a lot nicer than the dorms." Mike also went to a local four-year college. Michelle went to the local junior college, where she hoped to use the associate's degree to get a job as an administrative assistant, like her mother. Ashley, despite her high grades and test scores, went to a local business administration school that promised her employment in sixteen months. Understanding the vast socioeconomic terrain these students inhabit—somewhere between working and middle class—seems crucial to understanding the meanings of their whiteness, its privileges, and its relationship to literacy and its institutions. To get there may require relinquishing the socioeconomic and racial categories of analysis that literacy researchers have relied upon, a point Prendergast makes throughout *Literacy and Racial Justice*. In her race-inflected reading of Shirley Brice Heath's *Ways with Words,* for example, Prendergast examines how ethnographies can produce the "typifications" Abu-Lughod writes of, and she looks at how such typifications can inadvertently forward the notion of literacy as white property. In her analysis of the "absent presence" of race in *Ways*, Prendergast analyzes Heath's field notes and documents from her Piedmont literacy study and discovers how ethnography, like schooling, maintains white privilege even when it is ostensibly aimed at deconstructing it. Toward this end, it is worth remembering that Heath's pivotal study rests on the ethnographic construction of three communities, one black, one working-class white, and one middle-class white. The working-class community, as Prendergast points out, is described in ways that make it appear to be as different from the middle-class community as the Black community seems to be. But as Prendergast notes, "the history of desegregation in the area suggests that white mainstreamers and the white working class had an imagined community of their own—an identification based on race that crossed class lines. Schools were seen as mechanisms through which those racial lines might be maintained, even as economic disparities became starker" (85).

As my research ended, I came back again and again to the school's Web site and its claim that three-fourths of its students sought postsecondary education. When I first read that claim, I imagined, as perhaps the Web site's creators had hoped readers would, three-quarters of the graduating class heading off to four-year universities and small liberal arts colleges, the luckier among them to Harvard and Yale. In this way the claim creates an imagined community of middle-class whites, one that is, ironically, echoed in multicultural pedagogies that make few if any class distinctions in their descriptions of racial groups and, perhaps even more disconcerting, by pedagogies of whiteness that in their economically inflected critique of the power of white privilege also fail to address in any meaningful way the needs and desires of students like Michelle. Addressing such students will require getting beyond metaphors that equate white racial identity with tangible assets and moving toward seeing whiteness as a series of ongoing emotioned strategies and negotiations—as a process. What would it mean to bring this perspective, rather than McIntosh's "knapsack," into the antiracist classroom for students like Michelle; to teach white students about the power of their imagined community and to compare that power with their own experiences of privilege, with their struggles to attain it, and with their skepticism toward it? These are questions that must be addressed if we are to teach successfully against racism and if we are to disentangle the complex—albeit persistent—relationship between whiteness, privilege, and racism.

In addition, the questions raised here point to the need to examine in different terms ongoing debates about racial segregation and public education. My analysis of the racism I uncovered at Laurel Canyons strongly suggests that racism will not be ameliorated by increasing white students' exposure to difference. This is not to say that we should not work to end the educational apartheid Jonathan Kozol and others have so meticulously and painfully documented. But we should be clear that when we do end it, when we finally have public schools that reflect the diversity of our communities, white students may not be suddenly "cured" of their racial attitudes and beliefs. In the same vein, desegregating our schools may not have the assumed effect of offering students of color access to the same opportunities for higher education that white students have. Students are complexly culturally situated in relation to those opportunities. They are not tangible commodities that white students own in any felt sense. Again, this is not to say that offering students of color the same educational opportunities routinely available to whites is not an immediate moral and political necessity.

But we also need to understand that changing what is in whose knapsack may not address the emotioned ways students come to acquire racial identities and beliefs through processes of schooling. Changing racism will thus require more than ending material inequity. It will also require changing the institutional and discursive practices of schooling—the emotioned rules that schools demand and that give racist ideas their persuasive power.

The story of my year at Laurel Canyons represents the ongoing challenges inherent in critical pedagogical projects, as well as the ongoing need for them. The challenges are entrenched in a history of inequality and privilege that resists interrogation, revision, or transformation. The attention I've paid throughout this book to the emotioned dimensions of race holds promise for those of us who hope to teach our students to see the world differently. It shows us, for example, how we unintentionally teach emotioned positions and frameworks that work against other, more explicit pedagogical goals. It suggests the multilayered complexity of the consciousness formation that goes on via literacy teaching and learning, the complexity of the symbolic material that schools provide, via equally complex emotioned rules, and the relationship between those rules and race. I've tried to unpack the multiple paths across which discourses travel as they become persuasive to individuals and groups. And I've focused on how particular discursive forms come to mean, how they structure feelings or emerge from them, how individual and collective "selves" are called into being by them. My research at Laurel Canyons strongly suggests that students are not persuaded to take up particular racist discourses because of economic or social self-interest or gain, or because of ignorance or lack of exposure to "difference." It suggests, instead, that these discourses took root in deeper, more intangible places: in the heart, in notions of the self and family, in dreams and hopes of and fears about the social world and the student's place in it, as well as in more counterintuitive places: in the hidden lessons we teach when we try to motivate and control students, in the routine practices and rituals of our classrooms. Most of the students at Laurel Canyons believed that racism was wrong. They felt that injustice should be addressed and rectified. At the same time, as we've seen, they held beliefs and often made more careless comments that strongly suggested otherwise. If we believe that language constructs and reproduces social reality, that it is through language that injustice is created and sustained, then we have to take students' arguments and points of view and off-hand comments seriously. We have to take seriously those vexing moments of resistance and racism that mar so many of our classrooms. At the same time, we have to find more complex ways to understand the roots of that language, its persuasive and emotioned appeal.

In the final pages of his book *Rhetorics, Poetics, Cultures: Reconfiguring College English Studies*, James Berlin writes of encounters with criticism of his work and ideas. One critic, in particular, haunts Berlin: according to this critic, Berlin's error was that he had "grossly overestimated the influence of English departments in the lives of our students and the workings of our society. English teachers [the critic insisted] are in the large scheme of things just not all that important" (189). Berlin's defense of the importance of the role English plays in the workings of our society is worth revisiting here. He begins with the ways English departments and teachers participate as gatekeepers, labeling certain students as competent and others as not, influencing decisions about who will move on to higher education and who will not. I would add that the responsibility of this role extends to the representations of students we create and promulgate in our research, including our research on antiracism. But for Berlin, the real justification for investigation into the workings of English is the role literacy education plays in the construction of consciousness—"the shapings of particular kinds of subject formations in young people" (190). Literacy education, Berlin writes, employs "technologies of self-formation. . . . By influencing [students] to become particular kinds of readers and writers, we finally perform the job of . . . consciousness formation" (192). To use this influence ethnically, Berlin writes, we must engage in disciplinary investigation and critique to understand where our technologies of self-formation are working and where they go awry. Such understanding is central to any future that involves using the power of the classroom to create a more just, compassionate world.

This powerful articulation of the role of the English teacher and researcher has deeply influenced me and has deeply informed the perspective I brought to bear on my experiences at Laurel Canyons. But it is just this—the persuasive power of the articulation—that also gives me pause. I think of Richard Miller's description of the figure of the Freirean teacher as "our community's most cherished self-representation" (1998b, 12), "a story teachers like to tell themselves about themselves—a way to make it from semester to semester that preserves the teacher's sense of self-esteem" (15). What would it mean to open up for investigation the persuasive pull, and the emotioned resonances, of this story for us? As Hicks (2002) reminds us, the "texts" composed by educators are "rhetorical acts of meaning construction, as socially situated as any other" (136). More important, Hicks writes, the texts we construct—from teacher lore to formal research projects like this one—are "fictions,"—literary shaping of events through storytelling and other rhetorical practices. As such they "reflect our histories and aspirations" (136).

One of the most powerful discoveries, for me, over the course of this research, was my own investment in discourse, the deep emotional attachment I have to rhetorics that give the world a particular shape and meaning. As I untangled the emotioned roots of students' investments in particular views and discourses, I turned, inevitably, toward an understanding of my own: the ways certain texts and points of view make me feel, the ways particular discourses call forth my own beginning stories and memories: A racially divided third-grade classroom in southern Texas in 1975, where "slow" equaled "of color," where, on the Monday after my family held a garage sale, some of my classmates of color came to school wearing my old clothes, and I grasped for the first time a sense of the humiliations of race and class. A high school journalism assignment that led me to a dark apartment complex a half a mile from my suburban home, where recently immigrated Southeast Asians lived, sometimes ten or twelve members of a family sharing a tiny one-bedroom. How surprised I was to discover this dark place, sitting in perplexing juxtaposition to my own sun-filled home. The seven-year-old rage of the foster child who lived with my family for a time, when he was told by the social worker that he was being moved to another family. The sense of anger and injustice and pain that undergirds these memories, and the ways those memories in turn animate particular texts and discourses for me, imbuing them with meanings that resonate.

I also remember the moments in my education when I learned that there were different ways to feel about these events, where the rules shifted, when the texts I encountered—literary during my undergraduate education and then, increasingly, critical as I acquired my political identity in graduate school—helped me feel my experiences differently, persuading me of the validity of new interpretations and more progressive frames: less pain-filled and reactive, more empowered and critical. I've begun to encourage students to explore these unmapped psychosocial terrains, between their own structures of feelings, the lessons they've learned in school and out, and the views they articulate in class, in response to texts and authors who challenge them. By examining my own discursive investments critically, I invite them to do the same.

Classroom practice thus rooted in memory and affect turns inevitably to the situatedness of interpretation and perception, to the world inside every head, as Ruth Behar phrases it. In the afterword to *A Way to Move*, Lynn Worsham (2003) calls us to see that "all education is sentimental, that all education is an education of sentiment" (163). Indeed, she writes, emotion is the primary object of schooling, wherever schooling happens to occur. Such a view necessitates a different point of departure for those of us who hope that literacy education can play a role in eradicating racism.

It suggests a fertile middle ground, somewhere between the idealism of a Freirean vision of social change through classroom practice, the intractable institutional realities that shape our teaching and our students, and the dynamic, emotioned presence of students themselves. It suggests that we engage more fully with the emotioned rules we teach, whether we intend to or not, and that we work, from there, toward more persuasive rhetorics of social change.

APPENDIX
WORKS CITED AND CONSULTED
INDEX

APPENDIX
RESEARCH METHODS

Classroom observations, conversations with students, and interviews were audiotaped. I spent approximately five hundred hours with Elizabeth and her students. I took field notes during all of my observations and reworked them, supplemented with audiotapes, into narrative form as soon as possible after observations. I attended school events—football games, the fall musical—and collected all written materials generated by the classes: drafts, final essays, journals, assignments, curricular guides, senior project documents. Detailed consent forms were signed by the teacher, all students, parents, and the principal.

Formal interviews with students followed a "semistandardized" approach (Merriam 1988). Questions were formulated in advance, but many interviews retained an informal feel, as interviewees were allowed to wander from the questions and many responses were followed up with impromptu probes, questions, and reflections from me. Interviews took place during the term, usually after class or sometimes scheduled at a time convenient for the student. They generally lasted for one hour. I also informally interviewed students in class throughout the year.

General Questions

1. Tell me a bit about your background: where did you grow up? How would you describe your family? Friends? Community?
2. What are your future plans?
3. What are you hoping to get out of this class this term? Thus far, how would you assess the class?
4. How would you describe the stories and poems you're reading in this class? How do they compare to what you've read in other English classes? Which has been your favorite / least favorite so far?
5. How would you describe the other students in this class? Are you friends with any of the other students?
6. What kinds of experiences have you had in the past with multicultural readings, classrooms, or activities? When did you first begin to learn about issues of race? What was your first memory of learning about race? How do those experiences compare to this class?

Questions about Texts and Class Discussions

1. What does this text mean to you? What is it about?
2. What does this text tell you about the author and his/her feelings or beliefs?
3. What does the text tell you about _____ culture?
4. Is this text representative of the culture? Explain.
5. What is your personal response to the text?
6. Could this text take place where you live or help explain anything going on in your world now?
7. Is this a good text for an English class? Would you assign it if you were a teacher? Explain.
8. What do you think this text teaches students?
9. What is the author's attitude toward racism/sexism/classism in this text? Do you agree with him/her?
10. The teacher said in class that this text _____.
    What do you think she meant by that?
11. The teacher has said that texts are shaped by gender, sexuality, race, and class, and that our readings of them are also shaped by our own gender, etc. Do you agree? Can you give an example?
12. Have the readings shown you anything about race, gender, or class that you hadn't heard or known before?
13. During the discussion in class of _____, some students felt that the story was saying _____. Did you agree? Explain.
14. You believe then that _____ is true. How would you feel if you discovered it wasn't true?

WORKS CITED AND CONSULTED

Abu-Loghod, L. (1993). *Writing women's worlds: Bedouin stories.* University of California Press.

Abu-Lughod, L., and C. Lutz (1990). *Language and the politics of emotion.* Cambridge: Cambridge University Press.

Ahmed, Sarah (2004). *The cultural politics of emotion.* New York: Routledge.

Alberti, J. (2001). "Returning to class: Creating opportunities for multicultural reform at majority second-tier schools." *College English* 63: 561–84.

Anderson, V. (1997). "Confrontational teaching and rhetorical practice." *College Composition and Communication* 48: 197–214.

Anderson, V. (2000). "Property rights: Exclusion as moral action in 'the battle of Texas.'" *College English* 62: 445–72.

Applebaum, B. (2003). "White privilege, complicity, and the social construction of race." *Educational Foundations* 17(4): 5–20.

Banning, Marlie. "The politics of resentment." *JAC: Journal of Advanced Composition* 26(1/2): 67–101.

Barbalet, Jack (1998). *Emotions, social theory, and social structure.* Cambridge: Cambridge University Press.

Beech, J. (2004). "Redneck and hillbilly discourse in the writing classroom: Classifying critical pedagogies of whiteness." *College English* 67: 172–86.

Behar, R. (2003). *Translated woman.* Boston: Beacon Press.

Berlin, J. (1996). *Rhetorics, poetics, cultures: Reconfiguring college English studies.* Urbana, IL: NCTE.

Blee, K. (1992). *Women of the Klan: Racism and gender in the 1920's.* Berkeley: University of California Press.

Bloom, L. (1996). "Freshman composition as a middle-class enterprise." *College English* 58(6): 654–75.

Boler, M. (1999). *Feeling power: Emotions and education.* London: Routledge.

Bolgatz, J. (2005). *Talking race in the classroom.* New York: Teachers College Press.

Brantlinger, E. (2003). *Dividing classes: How the middle-class negotiates and rationalizes school advantage.* New York: RoutledgeFalmer Press.

Britzman, Deborah. (2006). *Novel education: Psychoanalytic studies of learning and not learning.* New York: Peter Lang.

Burke, Kenneth. (1969). *A rhetoric of motives.* Berkeley: University of California Press.

Cashin, S. (2004). *The failures of integration: How race and class are undermining the American dream.* New York: Public Affairs.

Cintron, R. (1998). *Angels' Town: Chero ways, gang life, and rhetorics of the everyday.* Boston: Beacon Press.

Clifford, J. (1988). *The predicament of culture: Twentieth-century ethnography, literature, and art.* Cambridge: Harvard University Press.

Crowley, Sharon (2006). *Toward a civil discourse: Rhetoric and fundamentalism.* Pittsburgh: University of Pittsburgh Press.

Cvetkovich, A. (2003). *An archive of feelings: Trauma, sexuality, and lesbian public cultures.* Durham: Duke University Press.

Damasio, Anthony (1999). *The feeling of what happens: Body and emotion in the making of consciousness.* New York: Harcourt Brace.

Daniell, B. (2003). A communion of friendship: Literacy, spiritual practice, and women in recovery. Carbondale: Southern Illinois University Press.

Delgado, Richard, and Jean Stefanic (1997). *Critical white studies: Looking behind the mirror.* Temple University Press.

DeVoss, Danielle Nicole, Ellen Cushman, and Jeffrey Grabill (2005). "Infrastructure and composing: The when of new-media writing." *College Composition and Communication* 57: 14–44.

Dipardo, A. (1993). *A kind of passport: A basic writing adjunct program and the challenges of student diversity.* Urbana, IL: NCTE.

Dyson, A. (2003). *The brothers and sisters learn to write: Popular literacies in childhood and school cultures.* New York: Teachers College Press.

Ellsworth, Elizabeth (1997). *Teaching positions: Difference, pedagogy, and the power of address.* New York: Teachers College Press.

Fairclough, N., and R. Wodak (1997). "Critical discourse analysis." In T. A. Van Dijk (Ed.), *Discourse as social interaction* (pp. 258–84). London: Sage.

Feagin, J., and Debra Van Ausdale (2002). *The first "R": How children learn race and racism.* New York: Rowman and Littlefield.

Fishman, J., Andrea Lunsford, Beth McGregor, and Mark Otuteye (2005). "Performing writing, performing literacy." *CCC* 57(2): 224–52.

Frankenberg, R. (1993). *White women, race matters: The social construction of whiteness.* Minneapolis: University of Minnesota Press.

Freire, P. (1970). *Pedagogy of the oppressed.* New York: Continuum.

Gallagher, C. (1995). "White reconstruction in the university." *Socialist Review* 24: 165–87.

Gee, J. (1992). *The social mind: Language, ideology, and social practice.* New York: Bergin and Garvey.

Gee, J. (1999). *Introduction to discourse analysis: Theory and methods.* London: Routledge.

Gere, A. (1994). "Kitchen tables and rented rooms: The extracurriculum of composition." *College Composition and Communication* 45: 75–92.

Giroux, H. (1997). "Rewriting the discourse of racial identity: Towards a pedagogy and politics of whiteness." *Harvard Educational Review* 67(2): 285–320.

Giroux, H. (2005). *Schooling and the Struggle for Public Life: Critical Pedagogy in the Modern Age.* New York: Paradigm Publishers.

Goffman, Irving (1967). *Interaction ritual.* Garden City, NY: Doubleday.

Goffman, Irving (1969). *Strategic interaction*. Philadelphia: University of Pennsylvania Press.

Gorzelsky, G. (2005). *The language of experience: Literate practices and social change*. University of Pittsburgh Press.

Greene, S., and Dawn Abt-Perkins. (2003). *Making race visible: Literacy research for cultural understanding*. New York: Teachers College Press.

Gross, D. (2006). *The secret history of emotion: From Aristotle's* Rhetoric *to modern brain science*. Chicago: University of Chicago Press.

Harris, C. (1991). "Whiteness as property." *Harvard Law Review* 106: 1707–91.

Hartigan, J. (1999). *Racial situations: Class predicaments of whiteness in Detroit*. Princeton, NJ: Princeton University Press.

Heath, S. (1986). *Ways with words: Language, life, and work in communities and classrooms*. Cambridge: Cambridge University Press.

Hicks, D. (2002). *Reading lives: Working-class children and literacy learning*. New York: Teachers College Press.

Hochschild, Arlie (1979). "Emotion work, feeling rules, and social structure." *American Journal of Sociology* 85(3): 551–75.

Holland, D., Lachicotte, W., Skinner, D., and Cain, C. (1998). *Identity and agency in cultural worlds*. Cambridge: Harvard University Press.

hooks, b. (1997). "Representing whiteness in the black imagination." In R. Frankenberg (Ed.), *Displacing whiteness: Essays in social and cultural criticism* (pp. 165–80). Durham: Duke University Press.

Hunter, I. (1988). *Culture and government: The emergence of literary education*. London: Macmillan.

Hytten, K., and J. Warren (2003). "Engaging whiteness: How racial power gets reified in education." *Qualitative Studies in Education* 16(1): 65–89.

Jacobs, D., and Laura Micciche (2003). *A way to move: Rhetorics of emotion and composition studies*. Portsmouth, NH: Boynton.

Kennedy, T., J. Middleton, and Krista Ratcliffe (2005). "Symposium on whiteness." *Rhetoric Review* 24(4): 359–402.

Kintz, L. (1997). *Between Jesus and the marketplace: The emotions that matter in right-wing America*. Durham: Duke University Press.

Kates, S. (2006). "Literacy, voting rights, and the citizenship schools in the South, 1957–1970." *College Composition and Communication* 57: 479–502.

Kelchtermans, G. (2005). "Teachers' emotions in education reforms: Self-understanding, vulnerable commitment and micropolitical literacy." *Teaching and Teacher Education* 21: 995–1006.

Kopelson, K. (2003). "Rhetoric on the edge of cunning; or, The performance of neutrality (re)considered as a composition pedagogy for student resistance." *College Composition and Communication* 51(1): 115–46.

Kozol, J. (2005). *The shame of the nation: The restoration of apartheid schooling in America*. New York: Crown.

Ladson-Billings, G., and W. Tate (1995). Toward a critical race theory of education. *Teachers College Record*, 97(1): 47–68.

Larabee, D. (1997). *How to succeed in school without really trying: The credentials race in America.* New Haven: Yale University Press.

Lakoff, G. (1996). *Moral politics: What conservatives know that liberals don't.* Chicago: University of Chicago Press.

Levine-Rasky, C. (2000). "Framing whiteness: Working through the tensions in introducing whiteness to educators." *Race, Ethnicity and Education* 3(3): 271–92.

Lewis, A. (2004). *Race in the schoolyard: Negotiating the color line in classrooms and communities.* New Brunswick: Rutgers University Press.

Lewis, C., J. Ketter, and B. Fabos (2001). "Reading race in a rural context." *Qualitative Studies in Education* 13: 317–50.

Lindquist, J. (2002). *A place to stand: Politics and persuasion in a working-class bar.* Oxford: Oxford University Press.

Lindquist, J. (2004). "Class affects, classroom affectations: Working through the paradoxes of strategic empathy." *College English* 67(2): 187–209.

Lipsitz, G. (1998). *The possessive investment in whiteness: How white people profit from identity politics.* Philadelphia: Temple University Press.

Lutz, Catherine, and Lila Abu-Lughod (1990). Introduction. In Catherine A. Lutz and Lila Abu-Lughod (Eds.), *Language and the politics of emotion* (pp. 1–23). Cambridge: Cambridge University Press.

Marx, S. (2003). "Reflections on the state of critical white studies." *International Journal of Qualitative Studies in Education* 16(1): 3–5.

Massumi, Brian (1996). "The autonomy of affect." In P. Patton (Ed.), *Deleuze: A critical reader.* London: Blackwell, pp. 139–61.

Massumi, Brian (2002). *Parables for the virtual: Movement, affect, sensation.* Duke University Press.

McIntosh, P. (1991). "White privilege and male privilege: A personal account of coming to see correspondences through work in women's studies." In Margaret L. Andersen and Patricia Hill Collins (Eds.), *Race, class, and gender: An anthology.* New York: Wadsworth.

McIntosh, P. (1992). "White privilege and male privilege: A personal account of coming to see correspondences through work in women's studies." In M. L. Anderson and P. H. Collins (Eds.), *Race, class, and gender: An anthology* (pp. 70–81). Belmont, CA: Wadsworth.

McIntyre, A. (1997). *Making meaning of whiteness: exploring racial identity with white teachers.* New York: SUNY Press.

Merriam, S. (1998). *Qualitative research and case study applications in education.* San Francisco: Jossey-Bass.

Miller, R. (1998a). *As if learning mattered: Reforming higher education.* Ithaca: Cornell University Press.

Miller, R. (1998b). "The arts of complicity: Pragmatism and the culture of schooling." *College English* 61(1): 10–28.

Min-Zhan Lu (1999). "Redefining the literate self: The politics of critical affirmation." *CCC* 51(2): 172–94.

Morrison, T. (1992). *Playing in the dark: whiteness and the literary imagination.* New York: Vintage Books.

Newitz, A., and M. Wray (1996). *White trash: Race and class in America.* New York: Routledge.

Perry, P. (2002). *Shades of white: white kids and racial identities in high school.* Durham: Duke University Press.

Pope, D. (2001). *Doing school: How we are creating a generation of stressed out, materialistic, and miseducated students.* New Haven: Yale University Press.

Prendergast, C. (2003). *Literacy and racial justice: The politics of learning after Brown v. Board of Education.* Carbondale: Southern University Press.

Quandahl, E. (2003). "A feeling for Aristotle: Emotion in the sphere of ethics." In Dale Jacobs and Laura Micciche (Eds.), *A way to move: Rhetorics of emotion and composition studies.* Portsmouth, NH: Heinemann.

Ratcliffe, K. (2005). *Rhetorical listening: Identification, gender, whiteness.* Carbondale: Southern Illinois University Press.

Reddy, William M. (1997). "Against constructionist: The historical ethnography of emotions." *Current Anthropology* 38: 327–40.

Reddy, William M. (2001). *The navigation of feeling: A framework for the history of emotions.* Cambridge: Cambridge University Press.

Reisigl, M., and R. Wodak (2001). *Discourse and discrimination: Rhetorics of racism and anti-Semitism.* New York: Routledge.

Rice, Jenny Edbauer (2008). "The new 'new': Making a case for critical affect studies." *Quarterly Journal of Speech* 94(2): 200–12.

Rich, A. (1996). "When we dead awaken: Writing as re-vision." In David Bartholomae and Anthony Petrosky (Eds.), *Ways of reading* (4th ed., pp. 549–62). Boston: Bedford Books.

Roediger, D. (1991). *The wages of whiteness: Race and the making of the American working class.* New York: Verso.

Rosaldo, R. (1993). *Culture and truth: The remaking of social analysis.* Boston: Beacon Press.

Rose, M. (1990). *Lives on the boundary.* New York: Penguin.

Schugurensky, D. (2002). "The eight curricula of multicultural citizenship education." *Multicultural Education* 10(1): 2–6.

Shor, I. (1992). *Empowering education: Critical teaching for social change.* Chicago: University of Chicago Press.

Sleeter, C. (1993). "How white teachers construct race." In McCarthy, C., and Crichlow (Eds.), *Race, identity, and representation in education.* New York: Routledge.

Srivastava, Sarita (2005). "'You're calling me a racist?' The moral and emotional regulation of antiracism and feminism." *Signs* 31(1): 29–36.

Strickland, D., and I. Crawford. (2003). "Error and racialized performances of emotion in the teaching of writing." In Dale Jacobs and Laura Micciche (Eds.), *A way to move: Rhetorics of emotion and composition studies.* Portsmouth, NH: Heinemann.

Solomon, Robert. *A passion for justice: Emotions and the origins of the social contract*. Lanham: Rowman, 1995.

Tatum, B. (1994). "Teaching white students about racism: The search for white allies and the restoration of hope." *Teachers College Record* 95: 462–76.

Thompson, A. (2003). "Tiffany, friend of people of color: White investments in antiracism." *International Journal of Qualitative Studies in Education* 16(1): 7–29.

Trainor, J. (2001). "Critical pedagogy's 'other': Constructions of whiteness in education for social change." *CCC* 52(4): 631–50.

Trainor, J. (2005). "'My ancestors didn't own slaves': Understanding white talk about race." *Research in the Teaching of English* 40(2): 140–67.

Trainor, J. (2006). "From identity to emotion: Frameworks for understanding, and teaching against, anticritical sentiments in the classroom." *Journal of Advanced Composition* 26(3-4): 643–55.

Trainor, J. (2008). "The wages of whiteness? Rethinking economic metaphors for whiteness: Literacy and life goals in an all-white suburban high school." In Stuart Greene (Ed.), *Literacy as a civil right: Reclaiming social justice in literacy teaching and learning*. New York: Peter Lang Publishing.

Wildman, S., and A. Davis. (2002). "Making systems of privilege visible." In P. S. Rothenberg (Ed.), *White privilege: Essential readings on the other side of racism* (pp. 89–95). New York: Worth.

Williams, R. (1977). *Marxism and literature*. New York: Oxford University Press.

Winans, A. (2005). "Local pedagogies and race: Interrogating white safety in the rural college classroom." *College English* 67: 253–73.

Worsham, L. (1998). "Going postal: Pedagogic violence and the schooling of emotion." *JAC: Journal of Advanced Composition* 18(2): 213–45.

Worsham, L. (2003). Afterword. *A way to move: Rhetorics of emotion and composition studies*. Boynton/Cook.

Zembylas, M. (2005). "Discursive practices, genealogies, and emotional rules: A poststructuralist view on emotion and identity in teaching." *Teaching and Teacher Education* 21: 935–48.

Zembylas, Michalinos (2005). "Beyond teacher cognition and teacher beliefs: The value of the ethnography of emotions in teaching." *International Journal of Qualitative Studies in Education* 18(4): 465–87.

INDEX

155

Jennifer Seibel Trainor is an associate professor of English at San Francisco State University, where she teaches in the graduate program in composition studies. She is a recipient of the NCTE's Promising Researcher Award and a member of the National Writing Project. She has published essays in *College Composition and Communication*, *Research in the Teaching of English*, and *College English*.